Sea Kayaking the
Baltimore/Washington, D.C. Area

Sea Kayaking the
Baltimore/Washington, D.C. Area

Michaela Gaaserud

This book is not intended to be used as a how to guide for kayaking. It assumes no liability for the safety or skill level of the reader and assumes that those embarking on trips referenced in this book take proper safety precautions while kayaking, are comfortable with paddling safety and rescue techniques or are paddling with a professional.

Although every effort was made to ensure that the information contained in this book was correct at press time, the author and publisher do not assume and hereby disclaim any liability to any party for any loss or damage caused by errors or omissions, whether such errors or omissions result from negligence, accident or any other cause. All forms of exercise pose inherent risk. The author, editors and publishers advise readers to take full responsibility for their safety and to know their limits. Before sea kayaking, be sure that your equipment is well maintained and do not take risks beyond your level of experience, aptitude, training and fitness. As with any exercise program, yours should be prepared in consultation with a physician or other qualified professional person. Mention of specific companies, organizations, or authorities in this book does not imply endorsement by the author or publisher, nor does mention of specific companies, organizations or authorities imply that they endorse the book.

Copyright © 2007 Michaela Gaaserud
ISBN: 978-0-9765498-1-9

Photo Credits: All photos were taken by the author with the exception
  of the following:
Andy Harrah (pages: 97, 98, 101, 102, 114, 115, 117)
Peter Gaaserud (pages: 17, 18, 20, 21, 23, 24, 59, 60, 67, 68, 84, 93, 94, 103, 104, 105, 137)

Rainmaker Publishing LLC
Oakton, VA
info@rainmakerpublishing.com
www.rainmakerpublishing.com

Acknowledgements

As the saying goes, it truly "takes a village" to put together a book. Thank you to the Baltimore/Washington, D.C. area paddling community for your interest and demand for this resource and to Werner Paddles and Current Designs/Wenonah Canoe for your support.

On a personal level, thank you to Renee for your creativity, friendship and hard work to pull this publication together and to Andy for your time, enthusiasm and technical expertise. Thank you also to Monica, for that scarce commodity called time, and most of all to Pete, for your love, support and for hauling my boat all over the country in pursuit of our happy place.

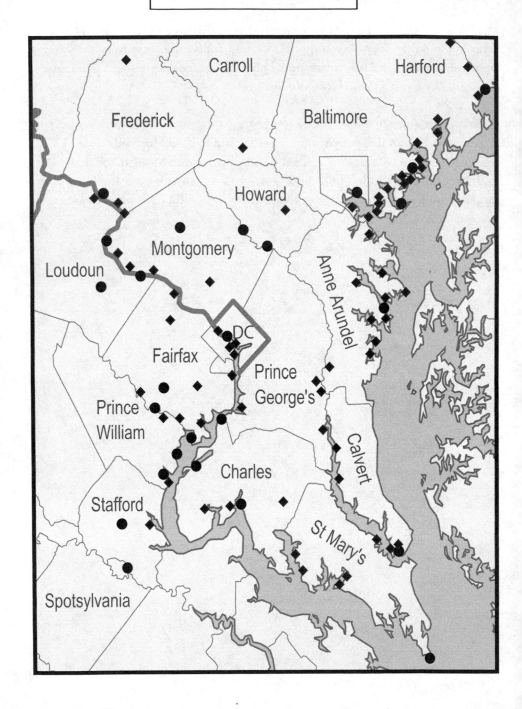

Featured Launch Sites
Additional Launch Sites

About This Book

It is no secret that a friendly rivalry exists between Northern Virginia and Maryland residents. I consider it more of a sibling rivalry since in reality the two states share many common characteristics in addition to borders with the nation's capital. One of these characteristics is a wealth of water. Tidal waterways, lakes and rivers are all easily accessible from any location in the region. The obvious choices are the Chesapeake Bay and the Potomac River, both which form boundaries between the states geographically, but the possibilities for paddling are endless.

I will set all rivalries aside and address the Baltimore/Washington, D.C. area as a whole, focusing on diverse paddling destinations that are easily accessible and worthy of a day of exploration.

The first seven chapters focus on two or more neighboring counties (and Washington, D.C.). Each contains in-depth descriptions of my favorite places to paddle in the counties for a total of 25 featured sites. In addition to these 25 sites, this book includes information about 67 additional launches with a brief description of the area, logistical information including the type of launch, fees, available parking and restroom facilities and basic directions from the closest major highway. The final chapter provides a list of local outfitters, paddling clubs and paddling associations in the region.

This book is not meant to be an all inclusive resource. There are additional parks and marinas that provide good water access in this region, but I selected what I feel to be a good sampling of sites spread along a variety of waterways.

Unlike many guidebooks that feature a specific route to follow, each destination featured in this book is suited for day outings of any duration. Paddle for an hour, or paddle all day — the choice is yours. I do not want you to skip a great destination because I show a 15-mile route and you only have time for a short paddle.

Although launch sites, fees and park regulations are subject to change at any time, many of the sites described in this book have existed for many years and will remain reliable launching options.

When planning your trip, keep in mind that what looks like a few easy miles of paddling can sometimes turn into a day-long adventure, depending on wind and water conditions. For this reason, be sure to dress appropriately and bring supplies for double the time you plan to be out.

Above all, keep in mind that this book is not a "how to," but rather a "where to" guide. The conditions of all waterways are subject to change throughout the year depending on tides, weather, and man-made factors. It assumes that readers observe proper safety precautions when paddling, are aware of current water conditions, have taken self-rescue courses, and are comfortable reading water, paddling in currents and paddling in adverse weather conditions. It also assumes that readers take responsibility for their safety at all times and never paddle alone.

Table of Contents

Chapter 3: Howard, Montgomery and Frederick Counties

Chapter 4: Anne Arundel, Charles and Prince George's Counties

Chapter 5: Calvert and St. Mary's Counties

Chapter 6: Loudoun and Fairfax Counties

Chapter 7: Prince William, Stafford and Spotsylvania Counties

Chapter 8: Paddling Resources

Introduction

A little more than a decade ago, people in the Baltimore/Washington, D.C. suburbs stared at the sea kayak on top of my car with a complete lack of recognition. While hordes of happy paddlers stroked the waterways of coastal Maine and the Pacific Northwest, I'd slip my kayak off the local boat ramps accompanied only by canoes and motorized watercraft.

I thought it was odd that in such a transient community, a sport enjoyed elsewhere in the country that was so friendly to people of all ages had barely appeared on the radar screen. Yet, time after time, I was asked, "Do you take that down Great Falls?" and "How do you keep from tipping over?"

Slowly, over the years, the inquisitive looks faded and the number of questions diminished as sea kayaking gained popularity in the mid-Atlantic region. I personally credit the outfitters in the beach communities of the Outer Banks in North Carolina and neighboring coastal areas for introducing D.C. and Baltimore area vacationers to the sport. It was where I first learned to paddle nearly 15 years ago, and the number of new paddlers there increases every summer. Whatever the reason, sea kayaking has taken a firm hold in Virginia, D.C. and Maryland and there are now kayaking outfitters, sea kayaking clubs and groups who enjoy weekly paddles together to relax after work.

If you are reading this book, more than likely you have discovered the sport of sea kayaking as well and are hoping to learn of new places to paddle in this region. I sincerely hope you enjoy this book and find it to be a useful resource to begin or continue your own exploration. I hope to see you out there!

WASHINGTON
D.C.

Fletcher's Boat House

Georgetown ● ■ Thompson Boat Center

ARLINGTON ■ Columbia Island Marina

Gravelly Point Park

● Featured Launch Site
■ Additional Launch Site

DISTRICT OF COLUMBIA AND ARLINGTON

GEORGETOWN WATERFRONT
Body of Water: Potomac River
Location: District of Columbia
Launch Type: Dock
Launch Fee: $5.00
Restrooms: Yes (portable)
Parking: Yes

After living most of my life in the suburbs of Washington, D.C., I thought I had experienced everything the city had to offer. Growing up, I ranked sightseeing on par with bee stings and going to the dentist. Visiting the city usually meant waiting in long lines in the summer heat to tour monuments I had seen many times before, or visiting museums during school trips to complete history assignments. As a young adult, my view of Washington changed and the city became a haven for nightlife on the weekends. This view was short-lived as I entered the working world and took a job downtown. The city soon became a maze of rush-hour traffic jams and a place of business and sadly, I rarely returned there for pleasure.

It wasn't until one day when I was in my early twenties, that I considered going into Washington for outdoor recreation. My husband suggested that we rent a canoe in Georgetown and paddle near the National Mall on the Potomac River. I tentatively agreed but thought that the city wouldn't be a very good place to paddle with all the street noise and tourist congestion. I figured we would try it once and probably not return.

Instead, the city I viewed from the Potomac River was completely foreign to me. Washington, D.C., to my amazement, was strikingly peaceful.

With the vehicle noise out of earshot, the only sound I heard was the gentle lapping of the current against my boat. The stress I was used to feeling while moving about the city was conspicuously absent. I felt as if I were looking at our capital with fresh eyes and, I was able to admire the monuments as they glistened in the morning sunlight.

We rented a canoe from Jack's Boathouse, which sits just upstream from the Francis Scott Key Bridge ("Key Bridge") and has become my launch site of choice over the years. Jack's is located at the end of K Street, on a slice of prime real estate along the banks of the Potomac. It has been in business since 1945 and offers canoe and kayak rentals, kayak lessons, launch facilities (low docks), parking and portable restrooms. A local group of Chesapeake Paddlers Association members, called the Pirates of Georgetown, meet there for a weekly group paddle throughout much of the year.

The boathouse has survived for many decades, despite steep rises in the real estate market and competition for water access. It also has two longtime neighbors worth mentioning. The first is the Potomac Boat Club, which was founded in 1869 and is the oldest rowing club in the Washington, D.C. area. The second is the Washington Canoe Club, founded in 1904 and designated as a District of Columbia landmark in 1973. Its attractive clubhouse was built by its members out of salvaged timber from local burnt out barns. The Washington Canoe Club has placed athletes on nearly every canoe and kayak Olympic team and played a significant role in the birth of flatwater canoe racing in the Olympics.

Paddling North Toward Chain Bridge

From Jack's Boathouse, the two obvious paddling options are upstream and downstream. The trip upstream takes you away from the city into more natural surroundings. It is possible to travel approximately three miles in this direction before the current and rocks hinder a comfortable paddle. Be aware that you can encounter strong currents at any point along the way, and in higher water conditions, you may be in for quite a workout or be unable to paddle at all.

Paddling upstream, you can see remains of the C&O Canal System (Chesapeake and Ohio Canal) that ran from Georgetown in D.C. to Cumberland, Maryland, and was used in the late 18th and early 19th centuries. If you look past the shoreline, you can also catch a glimpse of Georgetown landmarks such as Georgetown University.

This part of the Potomac is the local training course for numerous crewing clubs. The shoreline is reserved for canoes and kayaks but be aware of practicing teams coming by and of competitions that are sometimes held on the river.

There are several items to note on this section of the river, especially when water levels are low. The Three Sisters are a group of three rocky islands located less than a mile upstream from the Key Bridge. Several legends explain how these islands were named. One involves the alleged drowning of three Roman Catholic nuns who were then spit back out of the river to become the three islands. Another tale describes three Native American sisters who tried to swim across the river to escape a pursuing chieftain. The sisters drowned in the strong river currents and were turned into the rocky islands by the Great Spirit.

Approximately a mile and a half upstream from the Three Sisters is a group of sunken rocks that are only visible during low water. The area is known as "Hens & Chickens" and these little outcrops can cause some foul damage to your boat. Be on the lookout for this group of rocks, or stay to the middle of the river as you pass through the area.

Two miles north of the Key Bridge is a National Park Service concession called Fletcher's Boat House. Fletcher's Boat House first opened in the 1850s and is located in the C&O Canal National Historical Park. It offers boat and bike rentals and the sale of bait, tackle and refreshments. The water surrounding the boat house is called Fletcher's Cove and the spot is known to be excellent for fishing.

When entering Fletcher's Cove by boat, visitors are required by law to wear approved personal flotation devices (PFDs), and D.C. Harbor Patrols will ticket those who do not. Also be aware that there are many rock hazards in the cove.

After passing Fletcher's Boat House, you can paddle another mile to the Chain Bridge. As you make your way upstream, you will trade human companions for wild herons, cormorants and turtles as all signs of the city fade into the distance.

Paddling South to Alexandria

Although I have spent many happy days exploring the waters upstream from Jack's Boathouse, my favorite paddling trip is a one-way jaunt downstream from Georgetown to Alexandria, Virginia. Depending on water levels, sightseeing stops and the swiftness of the current, the nine and a half mile trip to the Belle Haven Marina can take a few hours or an entire day.

One-way paddles present a logistical challenge but unless you are up for a 20-mile roundtrip journey, I recommend dropping a car off in the parking lot at Belle Haven. If you prefer the challenge of the roundtrip, I recommend starting at Belle Haven Marina and paddling upstream to Georgetown so you can head back home with the current.

Launching from Jack's, head downstream under the Key Bridge and Route 29. After passing under the bridge, you will come to Theodore Roosevelt Island, which extends past the Roosevelt Bridge. You can paddle on either side of the 88-acre island, depending on whether you would rather see the monuments and D.C. shoreline, or you prefer a more natural setting. The island is a combination of swamp, marshland and forest and is a memorial to the 26th U.S. President, who was a conservation advocate. Native Americans originally used the island for fishing, but today most of the fragile shoreline is protected. Launching is permitted on the side facing Virginia where there is a rocky shoreline. Parking is available from the northbound lanes of the George Washington Memorial Parkway. From there you can also access two and a half miles of hiking trails and see a monument of Teddy himself.

I normally choose to paddle on the D.C. side of Roosevelt Island, mostly because I enjoy seeing the monuments poking out of the beautifully planned city landscape. An early morning or sunset paddle provides the best lighting for the large white structures, and it is hard not to marvel at the Washington Monument and Lincoln Memorial in front of you as you paddle toward the National Mall.

Between the Key Bridge and the Roosevelt Bridge is Thompson Boat Center. By land the center is located at the intersection of Rock Creek Parkway and Virginia Avenue but by boat you'll find it on the D.C. side of the river (left side) at the mouth of Rock Creek. The center offers canoe and kayak rentals, boat storage and rowing instruction.

Not far downstream from Thompson Boat Center is the Watergate complex, made famous by the Watergate scandal in the early 1970s. The Kennedy Center is not far away and is clearly visible just before the Roosevelt Bridge. At this point, the Washington Monument is in view, as is the Lincoln Memorial. After passing under the Roosevelt Bridge, it's just a quick paddle over to the steps of the Lincoln.

The Lincoln Memorial looks out over the Arlington Memorial Bridge, which is widely regarded as the most beautiful bridge in D.C. The bridge, in addition to being impressive to paddle under (you can not really appreciate the size of the structure until you are sitting under its belly in a kayak), symbolically links the North and South since it is aligned between the Lincoln Memorial and the Robert E. Lee Memorial (Arlington House). It has also appeared in more than 30 movies, including, *Mr. Smith Goes to Washington, The Pelican Brief* and *Planet of the Apes*.

My favorite time of year to paddle in D.C. is during the cherry blossom season in early April. Of course, the weather in D.C. doesn't always cooperate in the spring, but if you have a chance to take to the water while the puffy pink blossoms are out, seize the opportunity. Although you will not be able to paddle into the Tidal Basin by the Jefferson Memorial (located past the Memorial Bridge and before the 14th Street Bridge), the beautiful little trees can be seen throughout the area and the cockpit of a kayak is a prime viewing location, away from the crowds of tourists and traffic.

Opposite the Tidal Basin, near the Virginia shore, are Columbia Island and the Columbia Island Marina. There is a boat ramp there if you need to take a rest. This is also a good stopping point if you need to use the restroom (although in a pinch, with the help of a paddling buddy to watch our boats, I have taken out along the shore of the Franklin Delano Roosevelt Memorial to use the restroom facilities there).

Use extreme caution when crossing the river. The area between the 14th Street Bridge and the Memorial Bridge is an "open speed zone" so motorized boats can go as fast as they want. A nice side-trip to this route is to paddle along the backside of Columbia Island (the island is about one mile long). There is a narrow channel between the island and the shore and it is a wonderful place to explore and view waterfowl.

Continue under the multiple spans of the 14th Street Bridge past East Potomac Park. East Potomac Park forms a point (Haines Point) where the

Anacostia River flows into the Potomac. As you continue downstream, Ronald Reagan National Airport comes into view on the right bank. If you missed your opportunity to stop at Columbia Island Marina, you can stretch your legs at Gravelly Point Park, between the 14th Street Bridge and the airport. There are only seasonal restroom facilities but there is a boat ramp. Gravelly Point also provides a front row seat for watching planes take off and land.

Looking across the river to the opposite bank, you can see part of Bolling Air Force Base. The base no longer accommodates aircraft but it manages all Air Force activities that support Headquarters Air Force and other Air Force units in the region.

After passing the airport, Old Town Alexandria will come into view on the Virginia bank. Alexandria's history dates back to 1669, when the land was purchased by a Scotsman named John Alexander from an English captain for 6,000 pounds of tobacco. The city has certainly seen its share of history, and now offers visitors an interesting variety of dining, shopping, art galleries and cultural activities in a quaint yet trendy setting.

You will pass by Founders Park before paddling along the Old Town shore. Continue past the city dock (watch out for river cruise ships coming to dock) and the Torpedo Factory (which was used to assemble torpedoes during World War II and is now home to several art galleries and studios). Paddle under the Woodrow Wilson Memorial Bridge and around Jones Point.

Take out at the Belle Haven Marina in Alexandria—a little more than a mile past the Woodrow Wilson Memorial Bridge. There is public parking, a boat ramp and restrooms. The marina is owned by the National Park Service and operated by Belle Haven Marina Inc. It was founded in 1975 and is now home to the largest sailing school in the D.C. area. Kayaks are also available for rent.

When you arrive at Belle Haven Marina, you will find yourself a short distance from countless restaurants and watering holes in Old Town Alexandria. There are too many options to list all my favorites, but if good affordable Italian cuisine hits the spot after a long day's paddle, try Il Porto at 121 King Street. It was Old Town's first Italian restaurant and opened in 1973. Then take a convenient stroll around the corner to 101 South Union Street, and treat yourself to some Ben and Jerry's® ice cream!

Directions: Jack's Boathouse is located almost directly under the Francis Scott Key Bridge at 3500 K Street (also known as Water Street). From the Key Bridge, turn right on M Street in Georgetown and then turn right on

Wisconsin Ave. Turn right on K Street and follow K Street to the end. There is a sign for Jack's Boathouse on the left. For additional information visit www.jacksboathouse.com.

ADDITIONAL LAUNCH SITES

NAME: THOMPSON BOAT CENTER
Body of Water: Potomac River
Location: District of Columbia
Launch Type: Floating Dock
Launch Fee: $3.00
Restrooms: Yes
Parking: Yes (Metered)

Directions: (9:30 a.m. – 4:15 p.m. and after 6:30 p.m. weekdays and on weekends anytime – other times traffic flow is different on Rock Creek Parkway): From Route 395 North, cross Memorial Bridge and bear right in front of the Lincoln Memorial. Turn right on Rock Creek Parkway. After about ¼ mile, stay right toward Route 66/E Street/Whitehurst Freeway/Rock Creek. Follow the signs for Whitehurst/Rock Creek. Stay in the left lanes. Turn left at the intersection by the Watergate complex then right onto Virginia Avenue. Get in the left lane and cross Rock Creek Parkway at the green light into Thompson Boat Center.

Description: Thompson Boat Center is the only public boat storage facility in Georgetown. It was built in 1952 and has been in operation since. The facility is operated by Guest Services, Inc., a long-time concessionaire for the National Park Service. Water access is by floating dock with about six inches of freeboard.

Launch onto the Potomac to view the D.C. monuments or head downstream to Old Town, Alexandria. The center is closed from December 1 – March 31. Call 202-333-9543 for additional details. www.thompsonboatcenter.com

NAME: FLETCHER'S BOAT HOUSE
Body of Water: Potomac River
Location: District of Columbia
Launch Type: Shoreline
Launch Fee: None
Restrooms: Yes
Parking: Yes

Directions: Fletcher's Boat House is located at the intersection of Reservoir Road and Canal Road. From Route I-495, take the Glen Echo exit (to Clara Barton Parkway). Follow the Parkway until it becomes Canal Road. Continue to the park entrance (4940 Canal Road, NW).

NOTE: There is a tunnel with a seven-foot clearance near the entrance to the park. If you car-top on an SUV, you may need to select another launch site.

Description: Fletcher's Boat House is a nice jump-off point to the Potomac River near the city, but be careful of rocks under the surface in the area. Fletcher's is a full service facility that sells fishing supplies and operates a snack bar. They are open seven days a week from 7:00 a.m. to 6:00 p.m. This is the place to go if you like to fish. You might even run into a member of Congress or a Senator out for a guided fishing expedition. Call 202-244-0461 for additional information. *www.fletchersboathouse.com*

NAME: COLUMBIA ISLAND MARINA
Body of Water: Pentagon Lagoon/Potomac River
County: Arlington
Launch Type: Ramp
Launch Fee: None
Restrooms: Yes
Parking: Yes

Directions: From the Capital Beltway (Route I-495) in Virginia, exit onto Route US-1 (Richmond Highway) toward Mt. Vernon Highway/Old Town Alexandria. Turn right onto Duke Street (east) and then left (north) onto S. Washington Street (this turns into the George Washington Parkway). Stay on the Parkway until you pass Reagan National Airport. Pass the entrance to Gravelly Point. Columbia Island Marina will be on your left.

Description: Columbia Island Marina is operated by a concessionaire for the National Park Service. Launching for kayaks is free and the facility offers food and beverages at their café. Views of the Pentagon can be seen nearby. Paddle out to the Potomac River and head upstream to view the monuments in D.C. or downstream to Alexandria. Call 202-347-0173 for additional details. *www.columbiaisland.com*

NAME: GRAVELLY POINT PARK
Body of Water: Potomac River
County: Arlington
Launch Type: Ramp
Launch Fee: None
Restrooms: Yes (portable, seasonal)
Parking: Yes

Directions: From the Capital Beltway (Route I-495) in Virginia, exit onto Route US-1 (Richmond Highway) toward Mt. Vernon Highway/Old Town Alexandria. Turn right onto Duke Street (east) and then left (north) onto S. Washington Street (this turns into the George Washington Parkway). Stay on the parkway until you pass Reagan National Airport. Start looking right away for the parking lot on your right. If you are traveling southbound on the Parkway, you will need to turn around at the airport and head north.

Description: This launch area offers quite a rush, from above that is, since the runway at Reagan National Airport is just a few hundred yards away. Noted as one of the best places in the country to watch planes take off and land; all conversation will be silenced as a plane lands right over your head. Launch onto the Potomac River and paddle upstream toward the monuments in D.C. or downstream to Old Town Alexandria. Whichever course you choose, do not make it a full day because there is a three hour parking limit at the park (mostly enforced on weekdays).

CARROLL

BALTIMORE

HARFORD

Broad Creek Public Landing ■

Susquehanna State Park ■

Havre de Grace ●

Millard Tydings Mem Park ■

Otter Point Landing

Flying Point Park ■

Piney Run Park ■

Mariner Point Park ■

Hammerman Area ■

Cunninghill Cove ■

Porters Seneca Park Marina ● Dundee Creek

Maryland Marina ■ ■ Beacon Light Marina

Baltimore's Inner Harbor ● Cox's Point Park ■

Merritt Point Park ■

Inverness Park ■ ● Rocky Point Park

Southwest Area Park ■ ■ Turner Station Park

Fort Armistead Park ■

● Featured Launch Site

■ Additional Launch Site

BALTIMORE, HARFORD AND CARROLL COUNTIES

Special Note: Water and shorelines surrounding the Aberdeen Proving Ground and islands adjoining the installation are restricted due to weapons and ammunition testing and research. Aberdeen Proving Ground developed a boaters' guide to restricted water zones which should be consulted before paddling in the area. The Aberdeen Proving Ground's Restricted Water Zones map can also be found at: www.apgmwr.com/images/recreation/boatersguide.pdf.

HAVRE DE GRACE
Body of Water: Susquehanna River/Chesapeake Bay
County: Harford
Launch Type: Ramp
Launch Fee: $5.00 on Weekends, None during the week
Restrooms: Yes (portable)
Parking: Yes

How I managed to grow up in the Baltimore/Washington, D.C. area without knowing much history of the Chesapeake Bay is a bit of a mystery to me. As children of a geologist, my sister and I often visited the Chesapeake to hunt for fossils at Calverts Cliffs in the southern part of the Bay near Solomons Island. But my memories of these outings were mostly of combing the cliffs looking for ancient barnacles and wading gingerly  through warm knee-deep water, trying to avoid the jellyfish that crowded the shoreline.

My only other exposure to the Chesapeake Bay was on our annual family trek to the Delaware Beaches. As we drove our overloaded station wagon over the Bay Bridge, I'd jockey with our 75-pound Airedale terrier for the window seat. I would eagerly look out the window at all the sailboats and imagine how scary it would be to fall off the bridge into the whitecaps far below. It was hard for me to comprehend the size of the Chesapeake. The only water I knew of where the far shore was past the horizon was the Atlantic Ocean. On paper, I knew the Bay wasn't nearly as big as the Atlantic yet from the car window, it might as well have been.

It wasn't until after college that I learned more about the history of the Chesapeake Bay — and that was only by accident. I took a trip to St. John in the U.S. Virgin Islands to meet with an entrepreneur who wanted me to help write a screenplay about Blackbeard the pirate. Research for this project led me to the Bahamas, the Outer Banks of North Carolina, and eventually my own backyard – the Chesapeake Bay. Pirates in the Chesapeake Bay? I was surprised and intrigued.

Although Blackbeard was best known for his ruthless handiwork in the Caribbean, and his eventual beheading in Ocracoke, North Carolina, he often retreated to the Chesapeake Bay to repair his ship and prepare her for sea. He was not alone on the Bay. The tobacco industry thrived along the Bay shores for nearly 200 years, bringing with it explorers from all parts of Europe as well as a large population of pirates.

By coincidence, around the time I began researching the pirates of the Chesapeake Bay, my husband and I caught the sea kayaking bug. What followed were many weekend trips to check out Blackbeard's stomping ground in our recently purchased kayaks.

Early on in my research, my husband and I ended up at the northern end of the Chesapeake Bay in the beautiful little town of Havre de Grace, a site once seriously considered for the location of the nation's capital. Havre de Grace is located at the mouth of the Susquehanna River where it flows into the Chesapeake Bay, and we were thrilled with the seaside like atmosphere of the community.

Havre de Grace is located off Route I-95, on the southern side of the M.E. Tydings Memorial Bridge. Exit on Route 155 and follow it by the Susquehanna Museum and into the Historic District of Havre de Grace.

There are several launch sites in Havre de Grace. The first two are at the mouth of the Susquehanna River. My favorite is north of the train bridge at the intersection of Otsego and Union Streets (on Water Street at Jean

Roberts Memorial Park). This site features a small ramp, parking area and restroom facilities (there is a $5.00 launch fee).

The second launch is just downstream, off of Franklin Street by the Tidewater Grille (which is a great choice for seafood lovers after a long day of paddling). Launch at the small sandy beach alongside a rock jetty (no launch fee, no restrooms) and then park in the municipal lot (take Union Street or St. John Street to Franklin Street). There is also a third launch site at the Millard Tydings Memorial Park off of Commerce Street, about a mile away on the south side of town. This third site provides direct access to the Chesapeake Bay; the other two are around the corner, so to speak, at the mouth of the Susquehanna.

If you are new to the area, explore the shoreline of Havre de Grace by paddling south from either the Tidewater Grille or Jean Roberts Park. You will see quaint restaurants and shops from the water and you can paddle up to the lighthouse on Concord Point, where the Havre de Grace Decoy Museum is also located. If you continue past the town by the National Guard Reservation, you will see Aberdeen Proving Ground in the distance, jutting out into the Bay. You can continue paddling past several uninhabited islands, past the ancestral home of Governor Tydings (now a rehabilitation center for people suffering from substance abuse problems) and into Swan Creek (about five miles from town).

Paddling near the proving ground is strictly forbidden. In addition to getting a fine for trespassing, landing anywhere on the proving grounds can be very dangerous since there are live munitions. So, obey all signage in the area and respect the buoy markers.

Although kayaking along the shoreline is a scenic paddle and provides a unique perspective on the historical sights in town, I normally prefer to paddle north, away from town and up the Susquehanna River.

The Susquehanna is a beautiful river to explore and is also a vital contributor to the Bay. Fifty percent of all freshwater entering the Chesapeake Bay comes from the Susquehanna and it is the Bay's largest tributary. In fact, the Susquehanna is the 16th largest river in the country and is 444 miles long (its origin is Otsego Lake near Cooperstown, New York).

The Susquehanna is roughly a mile wide near Havre de Grace, and there can be substantial boat traffic on a nice day. Nonetheless, the shoreline provides some interesting opportunities for exploration.

Cross the river and paddle upstream to Garrett Island, the large island located under the Route 40 bridge (a.k.a. the Thomas J. Hatem Bridge). Garrett Island can be circumnavigated for a short leisurely paddle, or make an eight mile roundtrip paddle through the tidewater area of the river to Susquehanna State Park, located upstream from Havre de Grace.

The water near Garrett Island can reach depths of 80 feet. Water levels in the river can vary greatly both from natural occurrences and dam releases upstream, so be aware of rainfall levels and use good judgment before heading out. If the current looks strong, it is strong – save your paddle for another day.

In May, bird watching along the shores of the Susquehanna is at its best. If you enjoy scanning the riverbanks for signs of its feathered inhabitants, you can expect to see warblers, vireos, tanagers, flycatchers, thrushes and even orioles. For those more interested in creatures of the four-legged variety, be on the lookout for beaver, muskrat, turtles (painted and snapping), white-tail deer, skunk, groundhogs, raccoon, fox and the eastern coyote. The thick forest and large rock outcroppings along the riverbanks provide an excellent habitat for wildlife.

On a map the area looks congested but in reality the Susquehanna shoreline is lovely. As you paddle toward Susquehanna State Park and the Lapidum boat ramp, you will travel under several bridges and see remains of the Tidewater Canal that was dug along the riverbank many years ago to transport goods along the river. As you near the Lapidum Boat launch (located on the left shore as you paddle upstream), you will pass a granite quarry. Be aware of barge traffic coming and going from the area. Other than that, the scenery is tranquil and beautiful.

Susquehanna State Park offers historical landmarks and many outdoor activities, making it a nice turnaround point for your journey. Upstream from the park, the water gets very rocky and the Conowingo damn blocks passage entirely.

After a day on the water, I usually choose the Tidewater Grille or Coakley's Pub (on St. John Street) in Havre de Grace for a relaxing meal. The Tidewater Grille offers waterfront dining with good seafood. Coakley's Pub is a relaxing and often less crowded alternative with good pub food and friendly service.

Directions: From Route I-95 in Maryland, take Exit 89 (MD Route 155) toward Havre de Grace. Stay straight on Superior Street and turn right on Juanita Street. Turn left on Erie Street. Erie Street becomes Water Street.

GUNPOWDER FALLS STATE PARK - DUNDEE CREEK
Body of Water: Dundee Creek
County: Baltimore
Launch Type: Beach
Launch Fee: None
Restrooms: Yes
Parking: Yes

Even after years of kayaking the Baltimore/Washington, D.C. area, there are always new places to explore. Up until several years ago, Gunpowder Falls State Park, in Baltimore County was one of the much publicized places from where I had yet to launch. If you live in Baltimore County, the park is probably the most obvious place to paddle – I have had people tell me to kayak there who themselves have never lifted a paddle, but they knew it was where people go to do that sort of thing. After visiting it myself, I now believe the hype and it has quickly become one of my favorite places to introduce friends to the sport.

On a recent trip to the park, the wind was gusting to 25 mph, but it was a warm June day and the sun was out in full force. My husband and I headed to a new launch location for us at Dundee Creek Marina. Located in close proximity to Route I-95, the marina is easy to find and we pulled into the parking lot eager to get on the water.

Although the weather was gorgeous, the marina was fairly empty for a summer day. Everything looked nice and new, and I soon found out that the marina was severely damaged several years ago by Hurricane Isabel and much of it had recently re-opened. The building crew certainly did a fine job with the new structure and the atmosphere was very warm and inviting, as was the friendly staff working there.

We were pleased to find a car-top launch area on the right side of the parking lot, which had a lovely little sand beach with access onto protected Dundee Creek. There was no charge for using the launch (there is a fee for the main boat ramp at the marina) and we easily put our sea kayaks in the shelter of the creek, despite the gusty wind.

Another couple launched their kayaks just before us, and we followed them up the creek a bit past very large marsh reeds that housed a variety of birds including herons and redwinged black birds. Chatting as we caught up to them, they told us about the Marshy Point Nature Center, located nearby. It sounded like an interesting place to visit to learn more

about the area. After the usual chitchat about gear and boats, we left them to their paddle and continued on our own.

Paddling out of Dundee Creek we were presented with intriguing paddling options. Dundee Creek dumps into larger Saltpeter Creek, which ultimately flows into the Gunpowder River. You can easily spend a half day or more exploring the shallow water of Saltpeter Creek, viewing the wildlife and enjoying an extremely pleasant paddle. The other option is to head into the open water of the Gunpowder River.

We waved hello to a friendly, well-tanned fisherman who was paddling into Dundee Creek with a myriad of tackle and rods affixed to his sturdy recreation kayak. He looked intent on heading to his favorite fishing spot and shouted a hearty hello as he passed. Much of the shoreline along the creeks is private property, and a few property owners have constructed piers and duck blinds over the marsh.

Dundee and Saltpeter Creeks are ideal for beginner paddlers because the creeks are protected, yet those who want to try some open water paddling can do so at the mouth of the Saltpeter and the Gunpowder River (please see the note at the beginning of this chapter regarding paddling near Aberdeen Proving Ground). We did a bit of both; first paddling slowly up the Saltpeter, spotting several river otters and a variety of birds, then back out toward the Gunpowder River, where we saw a storybook perfect swan going about his daily routine as if we weren't there. We also saw an enormous turtle poke his blocky head out of the water several times to gauge our position before swimming off.

Completely satisfied with a wonderful morning of paddling, we took out our kayaks back on the little sandy beach and poked around the marina for a bit. The friendly people there showed us the high water line reached by flood waters from Isabel as she swept away the earlier marina structure. On the way out, we stopped at the Marshy Point Nature Center (7130 Marshy Point Road), recommended by the couple we met on the water. The stop was well worth the extra time. The nature center sits on 500 acres and is run by the Baltimore County Department of Recreation and Parks. The center has an attractive, well thought-out exhibit hall, an auditorium for audio-visual presentations and a decked area with picnic tables for the public (for information call 410-887-2817).

Dundee Creek is just one of several inviting places to launch a kayak in Gunpowder Falls State Park. Cunninghill Cove is another. After entering the main entrance to the park off Graces Quarters Road (there is a $3.00 entrance fee per car), follow the road into the park. On the right side of the road, before reaching the large beach area is a sign for a boat ramp in Cunninghill Cove. Although Cunninghill Cove is just a stone's throw away from Dundee Creek, this clean little launch facility offers a whole new paddling experience. The cove opens up to the Gunpowder River offering ample opportunities for open water paddling.

There is another good launch inside the main entrance to Gunpowder Falls State Park. If you continue past the entrance along the park road and into the Hammerman Area, you will approach a 1,500 foot beach area on the Gunpowder River. You can launch from the beach onto the Gunpowder River (just be mindful of the sections of the beach that are designated for swimming only). There is a seasonal kayak outfitter located in the beach area called Ultimate Watersports. They offer kayak instruction, rentals, tours and summer camps.

Directions: From Route I-95 in Maryland, take Exit 67A to Route 40 east. Turn right at the first light onto Ebenezer Road. Ebenezer Road turns into Graces Quarters Road. Continue 4.5 miles (pass the entrance to Gunpowder Falls State Park) to Dundee Creek Marina. The car-top launch is located on the right just before the main marina building.

BALTIMORE'S INNER HARBOR

Body of Water: Baltimore's Inner Harbor
County: Baltimore
Launch Type: Ramp
Launch Fee: None
Restrooms: No
Parking: Yes

Although located less than an hour's drive from each other, the waterways surrounding the cities of Washington D.C. and Baltimore are notably different. Now a major tourist destination in the mid-Atlantic, today's

Baltimore grew out of a well-established working industrial port, with direct access to the Chesapeake Bay. It paints a sharp contrast to the government-centric nation's capital, whose waterways serve mostly a population of pleasure boaters and cruising vessels.

Baltimore's Inner Harbor and the surrounding area boast a constant bustle of activity and the main tourist destination in the city. Although it has been a major seaport since the 1700's, tourism took hold in 1969 when the last all sail warship built by the Navy, the USS Constellation, was turned into a museum and docked permanently in the harbor. A series of urban renewal plans followed to make way for the redevelopment of the city. This allowed a multitude of tourist attractions, hotels and other businesses to take hold in the following years. The shipping industry still has a firm grip on the area, but Baltimore has more than its fair share of wealthy resident and visiting yachters of both the power and sailing variety. This makes for a very busy, but interesting, harbor and it is certainly worth a look by kayak.

I normally launch my kayak from the Canton Waterfront Park (next to the Korean War Memorial in Northwest Harbor). The park is easily accessible from Route I-95, offers free parking and is a well-positioned jump-off point to all the harbor attractions. There is no launch fee, and in turn, no real amenities (with the exception of seasonal portable toilets). However, the park boat ramp places kayakers right in the thick of things and is approximately three miles from the Inner Harbor by water.

The harbor is blanketed nearly end to end with marinas and private boating docks. In the span of a few minutes you will come across everything from the local weekend sailor to multi-million dollar cruising yachts from all over the world. Paddle to your right after launching for a direct route to the Inner Harbor. You will pass hundreds of boats tucked into their slips and, as you round the first dock you will even be greeted by a small replica of the Statue of Liberty.

As you can imagine, boat traffic in the harbor is substantial. In fact, it is one of the busiest places featured in this book, which is to be expected given its urban location. For the most part, the boats will keep to the channel in the middle of the harbor, but watch out for those entering or exiting the marinas. There is also a very active water taxi service that appears from around every bend. They do not hesitate to get close to kayakers, but fortunately, the ones I have encountered don't draw a big wake. Speaking of wakes – expect them all the time from every direction. I wouldn't recommend the area for training in a sprint boat, but sea kayaks shouldn't have too many problems.

As you paddle past the nooks and crannies formed by the marinas, you will soon make your way to the historic waterfront community of Fell's Point. Admire the nice shops and eateries from the water, but return after your paddle to stroll the cobbled stone streets, have a nice lunch, rent a bike or take a walking tour. The town was first established in 1763 and most of the businesses are still locally owned.

You can paddle around the City Pier and see some of the Baltimore Tugboats on the other side as you approach the Broadway Pier. If you pass by the Bond Street Wharf (off Thames Street) in Fell's Point, you will probably see one of the Canton Kayak Club's docking stations. Created in 1999 to allow people to better enjoy the natural resources offered by the harbor, this club is worth mentioning because of its unique and friendly setup. Club members pay an annual fee in exchange for free training and unlimited use of the club's kayaks and gear at four docking stations around Baltimore. Members are required to take a safety class before going out on the water, but then they can use the club boats for recreation or daily commuting.

If you continue paddling toward the Inner Harbor the size and grandeur of the power yachts and equally beautiful sailboats will seem to increase. Spend some time exploring, you can actually paddle under the city streets if you so desire, but I can not vouch for the cleanliness of the water.

Although the harbor is busy and it can be difficult to look beyond the garbage floating by (yes, the little blue boats cruising the perimeter of the shore are gathering trash), it is hard not to appreciate the view of the Baltimore skyline as you paddle into the Inner Harbor. So much work has gone (and continues to go) into the beautification and growth of the area that it is easy to get swept up in its fun vibe. It truly offers something for everyone, from elegant dining and shopping to the fabulous aquarium. I always enjoy the novelty of being able to paddle into this environment and soak it in from a unique vantage point.

Heading back out of the harbor, you will have a great view of the Domino's sugar refinery. Last time I paddled there, a giant freighter from Bombay, India was docked.

You can either paddle back to the boat launch the way you came, paddle the opposite shore past the industrial area of Locust Point to Fort McHenry, or continue exploring the outer reaches of the harbor. The shoreline seems endless.

No matter how often or how you choose to explore the Inner and Northwest Harbors, no two days will be the same. You may share the water with cargo freighters from exotic places or paddle by some of the world's most elaborate yachts. One thing is for sure, as the years go by more and more kayaks can be found in the harbor, exploring the shoreline, peaking under the city streets or transporting Baltimore residents to work.

Directions: From Route I-95 in Maryland, take Exit 57 (Boston Street). Turn left off the ramp onto Boston Street and continue over the railroad tracks. Turn left onto S East Avenue and into the Canton Waterfront Park.

ROCKY POINT PARK
Body of Water: Middle River/Back River
County: Baltimore
Launch Type: Ramp/Dock
Launch Fee: None ($5.00 Trailer Parking Fee)
Restrooms: Yes (at launch and on Hart Miller Island)
Parking: Yes

It was a tough choice. It was 70 degrees on a mid-November day. I looked out the window at the carpet of leaves covering my front lawn as sunshine streamed through the empty branches on the trees. Rake or paddle? Hmm, what to do.

The phone rang and the decision was made. A paddling friend, Andy, had the same thought and quickly convinced my husband, Pete, and me that we could not miss the rare opportunity to enjoy the unseasonably warm day. I fished a tattered list out of my dresser drawer and looked at the places not yet checked off, places I had hoped to paddle during the year but never made it to. My eyes fell on Rocky Point Park, in Baltimore County. That was it!

A short time later, we pulled out of our driveway, kayaks aboard, and waved to several neighbors as they raked and primped their suburban lawns.

Arriving at Rocky Point State Park, we were pleasantly surprised by the pristine condition of the park. Just a short drive from the city of Baltimore in Essex, the park had a distinct beach feel. The restroom facilities were closed for the season, as was the small sailing center, but we could tell (and confirmed on subsequent

trips during the summer months) that in the height of the summer, the place would be bustling with families, boats and picnickers. This late in the season, we saw several people fishing, but otherwise we had the park to ourselves.

Rocky Point State Park is located at the mouth of the Middle River, near where it flows into the Chesapeake Bay. There are two options for launching in the park. The first is a small launch area on a creek leading into the Back River and Hawk Cove. It is located on the right as you drive into the park. The second is from the boat launch at the end of the park, which puts you directly in Hawk's Cove. During the season there is a $5.00 trailer parking fee, but in November launching and parking is free. No amenities are available in the off season.

The tides at Rocky Point are very noticeable. When we launched from the oddly tiered dock (that did not have any tiers the right height for launching a kayak) the dock was fully exposed in the low tide. The neighboring ramp, which was also exposed, was too slippery for a secure launch in the cold water, but is fine when you don't mind getting a little wet.

The park sits on a peninsula in the river, overlooking Pleasure and Hart Miller Islands. We decided, after studying our *Maryland Delaware Atlas & Gazetteer*, to travel a triangular path from the launch site. The first mile and a quarter would take us to Pleasure Island and then we planned to paddle a half mile to Hart Miller Island, before returning about a mile and a quarter back to Rocky Point.

The distance on the map appeared to be just a few miles roundtrip but, looking at the islands from the launch, I would have guessed it was much farther. The view from the boat launch is confusing at first glance and I was very glad we had a good map with us. We could see both Pleasure Island and Hart Miller Island from the boat launch, but it was hard to tell how far apart they were. Distances can be deceiving around the islands, as can wind and currents, as we would later find out. The area is ideal for practicing open water paddling as kayaking to the islands requires several open water crossings.

Due to the late season cold water temperatures, we wisely opted to wear sprayskirts. After paddling this area in different conditions I recommend sprayskirts anytime of year, because of the potential for strong wind and waves. The water looked like glass as we headed out, but there was a slight wind sweeping across the surface.

The mainland forms a bay near the Rocky Point launch, and at first it is difficult to determine if the land opposite the park is an island or not. It is actually part of the mainland, and is a small community of homes with their own marina facilities at a place called Swan Point. We decided to head straight for the marina, and then cross the boat channel that separates it from Pleasure Island. Pleasure Island is easy to recognize since the Craighill Channel Range Lighthouse sits right behind it. This hard to miss landmark helped us get our bearings as we began our first crossing.

The crossing to Swan Point was very relaxing. There were few boats in the channel and we quickly paddled across the calm water to the houses on the far shore. We were joined by a variety of sea birds (mostly cormorants and gulls), that swooped and hollered as we came near, but really did not seem too upset by our presence.

Upon reaching the marina, we noticed that the water in the second boat channel between us and Pleasure Island was dark and rough. Upon further examination we saw that the water in the Chesapeake Bay, which was separated from us by Pleasure Island, had white caps on it. The wind, too, grew stronger as we headed for the island.

A few small fishing boats were in the area, but it was easy to time our channel crossing with their passing. Cold water splashed over my bow as the waves built, but we did not encounter anything overly exhausting. We were greeted by wide sand beaches on deserted Pleasure Island, a nice surprise that made us feel a million miles away from the city. The only thing missing was about 20 degrees on the thermometer and a margarita.

Behind Pleasure Island (which is a total of 27 acres), the Craighill Channel Range Lighthouse was clearly visible. It is one of the tallest lighthouses in the Bay and stretches up over 100 feet just off the island shore. A strong current swept between the lighthouse and the island, and Pete and Andy paddled just past Pleasure Island and determined that the current was too strong for a comfortable crossing to the lighthouse. Instead they ferried into the current and let themselves get pushed back toward the island several times for sport as the crew of a nearby fishing boat looked on. I pulled onto a small beach on Pleasure Island and sat and watched.

This is a good time to stress that the water around Pleasure and Hart Miller Islands often contains strong currents and surface winds. This is one area where you should only paddle if you are confident of your paddling and safety skills, or are paddling with a guide. As always, at least paddle with a friend.

When the guys tired of playing in the current, we regrouped for the crossing to Hart Miller Island. The wind picked-up and the channel between the two islands was visibly choppy as the waves sweeping in from the Bay intensified. Thankful for my sprayskirt, we began our crossing.

As we approached Hart Miller Island, we could see several trucks and a crane on the south side of the island. Hart Miller is home to a dredged sediment containment project that began in 1981. The machinery looked a bit out of place in the otherwise natural setting, especially since it was sitting on a piece of land surrounded by water.

We paddled along the western shore of the island and rounded the bend to the north side where we were greeted by a 3,000 foot long sandy beach. On subsequent weekend trips to the island in the summer, I've seen more than a hundred boats anchored there. Not so that day in November. We had the beach to ourselves. The park is a total of 244 acres and has camping, fishing, swimming, and even a few hiking trails. The island is accessible only by private boat.

The crossing back to Rocky Point was challenging. The waves steadily mounted as the wind continued to strengthen, and we surfed from crest to crest through the whitecaps. As cold water splashed over my head, I reasoned that this would be great fun in the warm water in, perhaps, July; capsizing today, however, would not be my idea of a good time. I looked over at Pete, who smiled and waved – clearly having a great time.

On our way back to the launch site, we had a clear view of the Baltimore County Sailing Center located in Rocky Point State Park. In addition to sailing lessons, they offer kayak instruction during the summer and escort groups to the islands.

Even with the challenging water conditions, we completed our triangular course in about two hours. On a nice summer day, it is worth making a day trip with a picnic and spending some time on the islands exploring and relaxing.

Returning to the launch, we noticed that the tide had come over the dock we launched from and much of the boat ramp. Taking out on the ramp, a bit chilly and a bit tired, we agreed to grab a warm lunch on the way home. Driving out of the park, we saw a sign for the Island View Waterfront Café – located on Island View Road. What a find it turned out to be. The atmosphere was relaxed (located right on the water) and the food was the perfect finale to an afternoon of paddling. I have two recommendations if you decide to dine there - try the Hot Crab Pretzel and ask the friendly staff about the episode of *Homicide* that was filmed there a number of years ago.

Directions: From Route I-95 in Maryland, take I-695 to the Essex exit (Route 702 west) to Back River Neck Road. Follow the road to Rocky Point Park.

The ramp is open daily at 6:00 a.m. and closes November – March at 5:30 p.m., April, May, September and October at 8:00 p.m. and June – August at 8:30 p.m. Call 410-887-3873 for additional information.

ADDITIONAL LAUNCH SITES

NAME: MILLARD TYDINGS MEMORIAL PARK
Body of Water: Chesapeake Bay
County: Harford
Launch type: Ramp
Launch Fee: None (for car-top launching)
Restrooms: Yes (portable)
Parking: Yes

Directions: From Route I-95 in Maryland, take Exit 89 (MD Route 155) toward US 40 and Havre de Grace. Turn right on Lewis Street, then left on Revolution Street. Turn right on Union Avenue and then left on Commerce Street.

Description: This is another good launch site in Havre de Grace. Paddle along the town shoreline and up into the Susquehanna River or paddle southwest along the bay shoreline. Call the Yacht Basin at 410-939-0015 for additional information.

NAME: SUSQUEHANNA STATE PARK
Body of Water: Susquehanna River
County: Harford
Launch Type: Ramp
Launch Fee: $10.00 for Maryland residents, $11.00 all other
Restrooms: Yes
Parking: Yes

Directions: From Route I-95 in Maryland, take Exit 89 to Route 155. Continue on Route 155 to Route 161. Turn right on Route 161 and then right on Rock Run Road. Follow Rock Run Road to the park entrance.

Description: Susquehanna State Park offers access to the Susquehanna River via the Lapidum Boat Launch. Havre de Grace and the headwaters of the Chesapeake Bay are just four miles downstream. Boat ramps at the park are open year round. Yearly launch passes are available.

NAME: BROAD CREEK PUBLIC LANDING
Body of Water: Broad Creek
County: Harford
Launch Type: Ramp
Launch Fee: None
Parking: Yes
Restrooms: None

Directions: From Route I-95 in Maryland, take Exit 77B to Route 24 north (toward Bel Air). Turn right onto US-1 north / MD-24 north (follow Route 1). Turn left onto Smith Road, the left onto Castleton Road. Turn right onto Flintville Road and continue to Paddrick Road. The landing is at Flintville and Paddrick Roads in Darlington. Call 410-638-3853 for additional information.

Description: The public landing is located on protected Broad Creek. Explore the more natural side of the creek by paddling west from the landing (the creek quickly narrows), or pass by neighborhoods to the right as you make your way toward the Susquehanna River, north of the Conowingo Dam (be sure to stay at least 400 yards from the dam).

NAME: FLYING POINT PARK
Body of Water: Bush River
County: Harford
Launch Type: Ramp
Launch Fee: None
Restrooms: Yes
Parking: Yes

Directions: From Route I-95 in Maryland, take Route 24 south on Emmorton Road (Exit 77A) Turn left on Edgewood Road. Then turn left onto Willoughby Beach Road. Turn left onto Flying Point Road and then left again onto Kennard Ave. Follow to Flying Point Park.

Description: Explore the backwaters of the Bush River. Stay clear of the restricted area surrounding Aberdeen Proving Grounds. For information on ramp hours call: 410-638-3572. See note at beginning of chapter on paddling near Aberdeen Proving Ground.

NAME: OTTER POINT LANDING
Body of Water: Otter Point Creek
County: Harford
Launch Type: Ramp
Launch Fee: None
Restrooms: Yes (portable)
Parking: Yes

Directions: From Route I-95 in Maryland, take Exit 77A to Route 24 south (Emmorton Road). Turn left to get to Pulaski Highway (Route 40 east). Turn right onto Otter Point Road (stay right at the fork).

Description: Otter Point Creek flows into the Bush River. You can easily explore both from Otter Point Landing. Stay clear of the restricted area surrounding Aberdeen Proving Ground. For information on ramp hours call 410-612-1606. See note at beginning of chapter on paddling near Aberdeen Proving Ground.

NAME: MARINER POINT PARK
Body of Water: Taylor Creek
County: Harford
Launch Type: Ramp
Launch Fee: None
Restrooms: Yes (portable)
Parking: Yes

Directions: From Route I-95 north in Maryland, take Exit 67A (White Marsh Blvd East) toward US 40. Take Pulaski Highway East (US 40) after approximately 5 miles. Turn right onto Joppa Farm Road. Turn right onto Kearney Drive.

Description: Mariner Point Park on Taylor Creek offers good access to the Gunpowder River. You can also access Days Cove in Gunpowder Falls State Park. This launch offers many options for exploration. Be sure not to paddle near the Aberdeen Proving Ground. For information on ramp hours call: 410-612-1608. See note at beginning of chapter on paddling near Aberdeen Proving Ground.

NAME: GUNPOWDER FALLS STATE PARK – HAMMERMAN AREA
Body of Water: Gunpowder River
County: Baltimore
Launch Type: Ramp
Launch Fee: $3.00 (park entrance)
Restrooms: Yes
Parking: Yes

Directions: From Route I-95 in Maryland, take Exit 67A to Route 40 east. Turn right at the first light onto Ebenezer Road. Ebenezer Road turns into Graces Quarters Road. Continue to the entrance for Gunpowder Falls State Park. Follow the park road to the beach.

Description: Launch on the sandy beach on the Gunpowder River. There's plenty of parking and kayaks are available for rent during the summer right on the beach. See note at beginning of chapter on paddling near Aberdeen Proving Ground.

NAME: GUNPOWDER FALLS STATE PARK – CUNNINGHILL COVE
Body of Water: Gunpowder River
County: Baltimore
Launch Type: Ramp
Launch Fee: $3.00 (park entrance)
Restrooms: Yes
Parking: Yes

Directions: From Route I-95 in Maryland, take Exit 67A to Route 40 east. Turn right at the first light onto Ebenezer Road. Ebenezer Road turns into Graces Quarters Road. Continue to the entrance for Gunpowder Falls State Park. Turn off the main park road to the right and down to Cunninghill Cove.

Description: Explore the protected shoreline surrounding Cunninghill Cove or out into the open water of the Gunpowder River. The launch is a quiet alternative to the beach area in the main part of Gunpowder Falls State Park. See note at beginning of chapter on paddling near Aberdeen Proving Ground.

NAME: PORTERS SENECA PARK MARINA
Body of Water: Seneca Creek
County: Baltimore
Launch Type: Ramp
Launch Fee: $7.00
Restrooms: Yes
Parking: Yes

Directions: From Route I-95 in Baltimore, take Exit 61 to Pulaski
Highway (Route 40). Take Martin Blvd (MD-700) toward Middle River.
From Martin Blvd, merge onto Eastern Blvd (Route 150) toward Chase.
Stay right on Carroll Island Road. Turn right on Seneca Park Road (918
Seneca Park Road).

Description: Launch at the mouth of Seneca Creek and explore
neighboring Goose Harbor Inlet and Hawthorn Cove. You can also
reach the mouth of the Gunpowder River and the Chesapeake Bay. For
additional information, call 410-335-6563.

NAME: BEACON LIGHT MARINA
Body of Water: Seneca Creek
County: Baltimore
Launch Type: Ramp
Launch Fee: $10.00 (closed Sundays)
Restrooms: Yes
Parking: Yes

Directions: From Route I-95 in Maryland, take Route 695 toward Key
Bridge. Take the exit for MD Route 150 East/Eastern Blvd (toward Chase).
Merge onto Eastern Blvd. Turn right on Carroll Island Road. Turn right
on Bowleys Quarters Road (825 Bowleys Quarters Road).

Description: Beacon Light Marina is a private marina facility that offers
access to Seneca Creek. Call 410-335-6489 for information and hours of
operation.

NAME: MARYLAND MARINA
Body of Water: **Frog Mortar Creek**
County: **Baltimore**
Launch Type: **Ramp**
Launch Fee: **$9.00**
Restrooms: **Yes**
Parking: **Yes**

Directions: From the Baltimore Beltway (Route 695), take Exit 36 (Route 702) to Eastern Blvd (Route 150 toward Chase). Pass the Martin State Airport and stay right at the traffic light onto Carroll Island Road. Turn right onto Bowley's Quarters Road. Turn right onto Red Rose Farm Road (at the sign for Maryland Marina).

Description: Launch on Frog Mortar Creek and paddle about a mile to the Middle River and on to the Chesapeake Bay or access several other creeks such as Stansbury Creek and Dark Head Creek. Maryland Marina has 360 boat slips, so beware of heavy boat traffic during the season. Call 410-335-8722 for more information.

NAME: COX'S POINT PARK
Body of Water: **Back River**
County: **Baltimore**
Launch Type: **Ramp**
Launch Fee: **None**
Restrooms: **Yes (seasonal with year round portable)**
Parking: **Yes**

Directions: From Route I-95 in Maryland, take Route 695 east to Exit 36 (Route 702). Exit on Eastern Blvd toward Essex. Turn left on Riverside Drive. Follow to the end (820 Riverside Drive in Essex, Maryland).

Description: Launch on the west side of Cox's Point Park onto the Back River. You can paddle around the point into Deep Creek and then into Duck Creek. The ramp is open daily at 6:00 a.m. and closes November – March at 5:30 p.m., April, May, September and October at 8:00 p.m. and June – August at 8:30 p.m. Call 410-887-0255 for additional information.

NAME: INVERNESS PARK
Body of Water: Bear Creek
County: Baltimore
Launch Type: Ramp
Launch Fee: None
Restrooms: Yes
Parking: Yes

Directions: From Route I-95 in Maryland, take Route 695 east. Take Exit 39 and turn left on Wise Avenue. Turn right on Lynch Road. Take the first left onto Kavanagh Road. Turn right on Jasmine Road. Take the second right onto Inverton Road and follow it to the end.

Description: Paddle on Bear Creek and into Lynch Cove from the public launch at Inverness Park. The ramp is open daily at 6:00 a.m. and closes November – March at 5:30 p.m., April, May, September and October at 8:00 p.m. and June – August at 8:30 p.m. Call 410-887-7536 for additional information.

NAME: MERRITT POINT PARK
Body of Water: Bullneck Creek
County: Baltimore
Launch Type: Ramp
Launch Fee: None
Restrooms: Yes (portable)
Parking: Yes

Directions: From I-95 in Maryland, take Route 695 east to Exit 39 (Merritt Blvd). Turn left on Dunmanway and follow it into the park.

Description: Launch on Bullneck Creek and paddle into Bear Creek. The ramp is open daily at 6:00 a.m. and closes November – March at 5:30 p.m., April, May, September and October at 8:00 p.m. and June – August at 8:30 p.m. For additional information call 410-887-7155.

NAME: TURNER STATION PARK
Body of Water: Peachorchard Cove
County: Baltimore
Launch Type: Ramp
Launch Fee: None
Restrooms: Yes (portable)
Parking: Yes

Directions: From I-95 in Maryland, take Route 695 to Exit 39 (Merritt Blvd). The road ends in Sollers Point Road. Turn left on Sollers Point Road. Turn left on Avodale Road, then left again on Rayme Road. Follow it to the park.

Description: There are four boat ramps in Turner Station Park. Launch into Peachorchard Cove and paddle on Peachorchard Creek. You can also reach Bear Creek. The ramp is open daily at 6:00 a.m. and closes November – March at 5:30 p.m., April, May, September and October at 8:00 p.m. and June – August at 8:30 p.m. For additional information call 410-887-7536.

NAME: FORT ARMISTEAD PARK
Body of Water: Patapsco River
County: Baltimore
Launch Type: Ramp
Launch Fee: None
Restrooms: Yes (portable)
Parking: Yes

Directions: From I-95 in Maryland, take Exit 49A to Route 695 south. Take Exit 1 toward MD-173 (before the Key Bridge) and turn right on Quarantine Road. Turn left on Hawkins Point Road and then left onto Fort Armistead Road. Stay left in the park (4000 Hawkins Point Road).

Description: Fort Armistead Park is a 35-acre waterfront park on the Patapsco River. You can paddle on the Patapsco or into more protected waters in Curtis Creek up to Marley Creek. The park is located at the tip of Baltimore City and also offers a picnic area and fishing pier. The park is open from dawn until dusk. Call 410-396-7931 for additional details.

NAME: *SOUTHWEST AREA PARK*
Body of Water: Patapsco River
County: Baltimore
Launch Type: Ramp
Launch Fee: None
Restrooms: Yes (in main park area)
Parking: Yes

Directions: From I-95 in Maryland, take Route 695 east. Take Exit 9 (Hollins Ferry Road East) and turn right on Daisy Ave. Turn right on Annapolis Road and then left on Georgia Avenue and continue to the end of the road.

Description: The water on the Patapsco River is shallow near the boat launch but downstream it opens up as it flows past Cherry Hill Park and Reed Bird Island Park. The ramp is open daily at 6:00 a.m. and closes November – March at 5:30 p.m., April, May, September and October at 8:00 p.m. and June – August at 8:30 p.m. For additional information call 410-887-1439.

NAME: *PINEY RUN PARK*
Body of Water: Piney Run Reservoir
County: Carroll
Launch Type: Ramp
Launch Fee: $5.00
Restrooms: Yes
Parking: Yes

Directions: From Route 695, take Exit 18 west (Route 26). Pass Route 32 and turn left onto White Rock Road. Turn left onto Martz Road and follow it to the park entrance (30 Martz Road, Sykesville, Maryland). The park is open April 1 – October 31.

Description: Piney Run Reservoir is a 300-acre lake located in southern Carroll County in Piney Run Park. Two boat ramps are available for launching kayaks and kayaks are available for rent. Gasoline motors are prohibited. Restricted areas include a dam and wildlife management area. The lake is known to have superb fishing. Call 410-795-3274 for additional information.

Featured Launch Site
Additional Launch Site

Cunningham Falls State Park

FREDERICK

HOWARD

Point of Rocks
Nolands Ferry
Monocacy Aqueduct

Centennial Park

Black Hill Regional Park

Triadelphia Reservoir

White's Ferry

Rocky Gorge Reservoir

Rock Creek Regional Park

Edwards Ferry
Sycamore Landing

MONTGOMERY

Seneca Landing

CHAPTER 3

HOWARD, MONTGOMERY AND FREDERICK COUNTIES

TRIADELPHIA RESERVOIR
Body of Water: Triadelphia Reservoir
County: Montgomery & Howard
Launch Type: Ramp
Launch Fee: $3.00
Restrooms: None
Parking: Yes

Our paddling trio had just completed a 30-minute "tour" of eastern Montgomery County by car. We were looking for Brighton Dam Road but neglected to bring good directions with us. We wanted to stop by the Information Center where launch permits for both Triadelphia Reservoir and Rocky Gorge Reservoir could be purchased, but were so far unsuccessful. Although my attention was mostly split between the road map and a dropping gas gauge, I did notice that the scenery was primarily strip malls and neighborhoods. There was no sign whatsoever of the natural surroundings I had heard about from other paddlers when describing the reservoirs.

Finally, after asking directions at a local gas station (and filling up) we headed down a winding wooded road and spotted Brighton Dam and the Information Center (located at the dam).

I was very surprised at what we found; or should I say, what we did not find as we pulled into the small parking lot. It was a beautiful summer Saturday and there was no one in sight, even though the Information Center had been open over an hour. There are no gasoline powered boats allowed on the lake, already a plus in my book, but I expected to find dozens of paddlers and fishermen getting ready for a day on the water. Only one lone car was parked, which presumably belonged to the park personnel inside the Information Center.

We walked inside the center and were immediately greeted by a very friendly ranger. After paying $3.00 each for our "Watershed Use Permits" (seasonal permits are also available), he provided us with an excellent map and brochure on our destination – Triadelphia Reservoir. There were also helpful charts posted on the wall, which gave information on area fish and wildlife.

Although water levels during the summer are normally at their lowest, since the trees along the feeder creeks to the reservoir soak up more water from the ground during their active growing season, the ranger told us that the water was actually much higher than normal due to recent heavy rain. He then gave us directions to the nearest boat ramp at the Greenbridge Boat Landing.

Piling back into the car, we followed the directions down a wooded road to the boat launch. There were several houses along the road, but the entrance to the landing was marked with a gate. A large rabbit ran in front of the car, stopped when our tires skidded on the gravel, then bounded into the woods. With the exception of our car noise, all we heard were birds chirping (the area is known to be excellent for birding).

The boat ramp was empty. We leisurely untied our boats and got our gear ready. There is a small parking lot near the boat ramp but no restroom facilities. I had asked the ranger to use what seemed to be a private bathroom back at the Information Center, and thankfully he had let me do so.

We were delighted to see that the reservoir lives up to its reputation; it is beautiful. It straddles the county line between Montgomery and Howard Counties, but its shore is void of any sign of nearby suburban sprawl. Triadelphia and neighboring Rocky Gorge Reservoir are surrounded by 6,000 acres of wooded land in the Patuxent watershed.

Triadelphia stretches northwest from the Greenbridge Landing. It is about five miles long and covers approximately 800 acres. If you explore all the nooks and crannies along the shoreline, your paddle distance can be much greater – so a full day on the water is a realistic goal.

Brighton Dam is visible in the distance from the landing (look to the right). It is 60 feet tall and you can drive over it on Brighton Dam Road. You can paddle toward the dam, but there is a safety line of buoys that should be respected. Don't approach them by kayak or you could end up fighting a strong current.

We paddled northwest (left) from the boat ramp into the widest part of the reservoir. The day was windless. We glided through the sunshine with barely a ripple. Triadelphia is mostly wide and tree-lined but it narrows considerably toward the northern end where rocky cliffs bump up against the water.

Colorful canoes and kayaks line the reservoir banks in many places, as nearby residents take advantage of the opportunity to store their boats there during the season (there's a mooring fee to do so). The large number of boats "moored" seemed grossly disproportional to the small number we saw on the water. In many trips I've made to the reservoir since, the same holds true.

As we approached the northern end of the reservoir, we paddled up an arm to the Pig Tail Branch launch site (there are four launch sites total, Triadelphia Lake Road, Greenbridge, Pig Tail Branch and Big Branch). We noticed a sign submerged in the water, not too far from the launch. Paddling up to it, I could read "end of boat ramp." Okay, so the ranger wasn't kidding when he said the water levels were high. The reservoir normally reaches a depth of 65 feet, but judging by the flooded shoreline at the top of the lake, I guessed it might have gained a few feet with the recent rain.

Flood waters at the northern end, where it is generally most shallow, circled trees that normally sit on shore, and we could paddle around their trunks and through the underbrush. It was an unusual sight, but I found it a little creepy as the branches reached into the still water and, although I didn't see any, I figured it would be a very nice habitat for snakes.

We saw a few friendly people fishing on the water in small, battery powered boats, but otherwise we only met a handful of other kayakers quietly enjoying the gorgeous day.

On our return trip we spent a lot of time exploring the nooks and crannies of the shoreline, adding substantial mileage to our trip. At Triadelphia, you can paddle most of the day without getting bored or having to retrace your route. Both shorelines are interesting and are worth inspection on an out-

and-back trip. We also had a nice opportunity to get some terrific exercise as the water opened up approaching our launch at Greenbridge. We topped out our speed at just over five miles an hour in our fiberglass sea kayaks.

Each season brings changes to the scenery at the reservoir. Springtime reveals the vibrant colors of thousands of azaleas planted in the late 1940's (mostly near the Information Center). Today some reach more than eight feet tall. Summer brings many warm days with still water. The changing leaves in the fall reflect the beauty seen throughout the Baltimore/ Washington, D.C. area, especially on a cool clear day when the summer humidity is long gone.

During the summer of 2006, Brighton Dam underwent repair work that required extremely low water levels in order for workers to adequately reach a section of the dam. Views of the low water were quite a contrast to my first visit during flood stages, and the boat launch was closed at the time. Wide sandy shores rimmed the lake and the boat ramps were completely exposed.

I have found that most any day is a good day to paddle the calm, empty water on Triadelphia. Windy days can provide a bit of a challenge in the wider sections and there are a few rocks to navigate, but all in all I find it to be one of the most enjoyable places to paddle in the region.

Directions: To the Brighton Dam Information Center: From I-270 north in Maryland, take Exit 5 (Route 189 Falls Road). Merge onto Great Falls Road (189 north). Turn left to stay on Great Falls Road. Turn right onto West Jefferson Street (Route 28) for about a mile, and then turn left onto First Street to continue on 28 east. Turn left onto Georgia Ave (Route 97 north) and after about 5 miles, turn right onto Market Street. Market Street becomes Brighton Dam Road. Turn right to stay on Brighton Dam Road (the Information Center is located at 2 Brighton Dam Road, Brookville, Maryland 20833). The center is open from 8:00 a.m. – 8:00 p.m., including holidays and weekends. Launching is permitted from March 1 – December 15. For additional information call 301-774-9124.

From the Brighton Dam Information Center to Greenbridge Landing: Turn left onto Brighton Dam Road, then right onto New Hampshire Ave. Turn right on Greenbridge. Follow to Greenbridge Boat Landing.

To the Pig Tail Launch: From Route I-95 in Maryland, take Exit 38 to Route 32 west and follow it to Clarkesville Pike (Route 108). Turn left on Clarkesville Pike and then bear right immediately on Brighton Dam Road. Continue on Brighton Dam Road all the way to the Information Center, or to go right to the Pig Tail Launch Site, turn right onto Ten Oaks Road and then left onto Triadelphia Mill Road. Follow Triadelphia Mill Road to Green Bridge Road and turn left. Follow Green Bridge Road to the launch site.

To the Triadelphia Lake Road Launch: From I-95 in Maryland, take Exit 38 to Route 32 west and follow it to Clarkesville Pike (Route 108). Turn left on Clarkesville Pike and then bear right immediately on Brighton Dam Road. Cross the dam (by the Information Center) and continue to New Hampshire Avenue. Turn right on New Hampshire Avenue and follow to Georgia Avenue (Route 97). Turn right on Georgia Avenue, then right again on Triadelphia Lake Road. Follow to the launch site.

To the Big Branch Launch Site: From I-95 in Maryland, take Exit 38 to Route 32 west and follow it to Clarkesville Pike (Route 108). Turn left on Clarkesville Pike and then bear right immediately on Brighton Dam Road. Continue on Brighton Dam Road to the Information Center, or turn right onto Ten Oaks Road, then left onto Triadelphia Mill Road. Follow Triadelphia Mill Road to the launch site.

ROCKY GORGE RESERVOIR
Body of Water: Rocky Gorge Reservoir
County: Montgomery & Howard
Launch Type: Ramp
Launch Fee: $3.00 (seasonal permits available)
Restrooms: Yes (portable)
Parking: Yes

Just four miles away from Triadelphia Reservoir is her sister lake, Rocky Gorge Reservoir. Longer and narrower, Rocky Gorge gives Triadelphia a good run for the money in terms of beauty and accessibility. I can't say for sure which one I like better, both are special in their own way. Apart from both providing water to 500,000 Prince George's and Montgomery County residents, and sharing the Information Center on Brighton Dam Road for the purchase of launch permits, they are very much their own destinations.

Like Triadelphia Reservoir, Rocky Gorge Reservoir is a dammed portion of the Patuxent River. It is approximately eight miles long. Like its neighbor, it covers 800 acres, but it has nearly twice the depth of Triadelphia. The Howard Duckett Dam at the southern end, is where water is pumped to the Patuxent Water Filtration Plant in Laurel, Maryland (you can see the

dam from Route I-95). The Washington Suburban Sanitary Commission (WSSC) maintains the reservoir.

Rocky Gorge can be accessed from three launch sites. One is located at the Northern end at the ramp by Brown's Bridge (off Brown's Bridge Road), and two are located at the southern end in Laurel (Scott's Cove and the Supplee Boat Launch). I normally launch by Brown's Bridge where the lake is very narrow. I should mention that the boat landing at Brown's Bridge gets pretty muddy in low water, so be sure to poke the ground with your paddle before you step into the water to enter your boat, I've come close to losing my paddling booties more than once.

As with Triadelphia Reservoir, local residents can keep their canoe or kayak at the reservoir along the banks by Scott's Cove for a fee.

I dabble in kayak marathon racing, and when I need to train, Rocky Gorge usually tops my list of places to work out. It is long and narrow, with just enough turns to be interesting. It more closely resembles a river than a lake. It is also fairly empty. I usually just see a few other kayaks and small fishing boats out on the water (no power boats are allowed).

If you are a bird watcher, this is the place for you. Rocky Gorge Reservoir is one of the few inland waterways with birds not readily seen elsewhere in the region. Sure, Rocky Gorge offers mass numbers of Blue Heron, a healthy population of osprey, and even a few bald eagles, but on a recent outing I spotted a Green Heron, which are only in the area during the summer months. I also see Killdeer regularly. They live in the region year round, but I rarely see them while kayaking. There is a buffer of woods around the reservoir that is owned and maintained by the WSSC. One of the reasons for the extensive bird population is that the trees come right down to the water, providing perches, nesting area and camouflage.

If you put-in at Brown's Bridge and paddle to the left, rather than out to the main part of the reservoir, you can make your way through a marshy stream area. On several occasions during low water, I've seen large flocks of Canada Geese on the mud flats that are exposed as the water recedes.

Although the Rocky Gorge shoreline does not appear to be as steep as you might expect from something with the word "gorge" in its name, there is more to it than meets the eye above the surface. Although it's less than a quarter of a mile wide in most places, it can reach depths of around 120 feet. Water levels can change fairly quickly in the reservoir, based on the local rainfall. Things can look dramatically different after a dry spell or a period of excessive rain.

There are several small arms that can be explored off the main part of the lake, if you want to add more mileage to your paddling day or spend some time scanning the shoreline for animals. I like to save at least one detour for my return trip to Brown's Bridge, to see something a little different on my way back to the launch.

I was surprised to learn that there are no natural lakes in Maryland. Without the creation of reservoirs, it would be difficult to provide water to the many homes and businesses in the state. The Washington Suburban Sanitary Commission, which is more than 80 years old, created both Rocky Gorge Reservoir and Triadelphia Reservoir and is still responsible for maintaining them today.

Directions: To the Brighton Dam Information Center: From I-270 north in Maryland, take Exit 5 (Route 189 Falls Road). Merge onto Great Falls Road (189 north). Turn left to stay on Great Falls Road. Turn right onto West Jefferson Street (Route 28) for about a mile, and then turn left onto First Street to continue on 28 east. Turn left onto Georgia Ave (Route 97 north) and after about 5 miles, turn right onto Market Street. Market Street becomes Brighton Dam Road. Turn right to stay on Brighton Dam Road (the Information Center is located at 2 Brighton Dam Road, Brookville, Maryland 20833). The center is open from 8:00 a.m. – 8:00 p.m., including holidays and weekends. Launching is permitted from March 1 – December 15. For additional information call 301-774-9124.

Brown's Bridge Launch: From Route 29, take Exit 13 to Route 216 west. Turn left onto Lime Kiln Road at the fork and follow Lime Kiln Road to a stop sign. Turn left on Brown's Bridge Road. The ramp is on the left (about a half mile up).

Scott's Cove Launch: From Route I-95, take Exit 35 (Route 216 west) and turn left onto Leishear Road. Turn right at the stop sign and then take the first left. The parking area is on your left (pass the first lot and go to the second).

Supplee Boat Launch: From Route I-95, take Exit 33 west to Route 198 (Sandy Spring Road). Turn right onto Bond Mill Road. Follow to Brooklyn Bridge Road. Turn right on Brooklyn Bridge Road then make an immediate left onto Supplee Lane. Follow to the launch site.

BLACK HILL REGIONAL PARK
Body of Water: Little Seneca Lake
County: Montgomery
Launch Type: Ramp/Beach
Launch Fee: $5.00 (season pass available)
Restrooms: Yes (portable)
Parking: Yes

"I've never seen so many kayaks in one place. The scenery is great and the people are unusually friendly."
That was how a friend described Little Seneca Lake in Black Hill Regional Park near Germantown, Maryland. It sounded good to me, so I persuaded another friend to skip out of work on a sunny afternoon in May and explore it with me.

Black Hill Regional Park is easy to find. It is near the Father Hurley Boulevard exit (Exit 16) on Route I-270. As is usual for me, I passed by the park entrance once before seeing it, but it is not especially difficult to find. There are two boating areas in the 1,843-acre park, a launch area for personal watercraft and a separate boat rental and recreation area.

We pulled into the boat launch area and found a nice wide ramp, as well as a sandy beach for launching. Along the beach and surrounding grass field were dozens of canoes and kayaks, clearly housed there permanently.

The thing that struck me most about the park was how clean it was. Granted, my first exploration of the area was early in the season, but even the portable toilet near the launch area was "clean" which, by my own definition, normally doesn't apply to any lavatory facility that can be moved. It even had a maintenance schedule posted neatly on the back of the door.

There was ample parking, and a bulletin board was posted with helpful information about the lake. The launch fee was $5.00 on the honor system (seasonal permits are also available). After depositing our cash and chatting briefly with an older gentleman who was hauling his fishing boat onto a trailer, we were soon on the water.

Little Seneca Lake is 505 acres and contains 15 miles of shoreline. The average depth of the lake is 24 feet, although it has a maximum depth of nearly 70 feet. Judging by the multitude of kayaks housed there and the number of paddlers I saw in the middle of the afternoon on a school day, I would say it is a pretty well-known local flat water destination. The park is beautifully kept with clean grounds and nice facilities and the people I encountered were, as my friend had said, all extremely friendly. We immediately encountered two fishermen who waved with large grins and shouted, "now that really looks like fun!" We waved back, gave them the thumbs up and paddled out toward the far end of the lake.

The lake is primarily tree lined. It has several arms sticking out of a loosely defined interior. To a newcomer, it can be difficult to figure out exactly where the main part of the lake is. It turned out that all the arms are worth exploring. One takes you to the dam while another leads you under the Route 121 overpass to a very quiet cove on the lake. The cove is filled with eerie looking tree trunks that are no doubt the remains of a forest that was flooded during the creation of the reservoir. We paddled around the trees, which are now bare with gnarly branches sticking out withered and gray.

The tree trunks provided an ideal habitat for wildlife. Everywhere we looked we saw turtles sunbathing on the many logs sunken around the edge of the water. We counted more than 100 of them in all sizes. They were stacked three and four rows deep, covering the log surfaces. As we approached, one by one they plopped into the water, watchful of us, but not overly afraid.

We spent more than an hour poking around the shoreline of the cove, looking for wildlife and studying the remains of the trees.

Paddling back toward the launch area, we passed by a half dozen residences along the shoreline before traveling under the overpass again. We heard a train's whistle blow in the not too far distance, but never saw the train itself. For the most part, the paddle was very relaxing and quiet.

After returning from our paddle, we drove around the park to the Visitors Center. The facility was very nicely kept and offered boat rentals during the summer. Boats are allowed on the lake between March 1 and December 15. The park also has many planned events, including night fishing outings (normally all boats must be off the lake before sunset). There is also a local group of kayakers from the Chesapeake Paddlers Association (CPA) who meet there once a week in the summer to paddle.

Directions: From Route I-270 north in Maryland, exit on Route 27 east (Father Hurley Boulevard) and turn left onto Route 355 (Frederick Road). Turn left onto West Old Baltimore Road and follow the signs approximately four miles to the park (on the left).

WHITE'S FERRY
Body of Water: Potomac River
County: Montgomery
Launch Type: Ramp
Launch Fee: $5.00
Restrooms: Yes
Parking: Yes

Just 36 miles up the Potomac River from Washington, D.C., is the opportunity to take part in a tradition dating back more than 200 years. It is hard to believe that the small, privately owned White's Ferry has made the short crossing between the banks of Virginia and Maryland literally hundreds of thousands of times and also that it has weathered decades of economic growth on both shores.

When it opened, the ferry was called Conrad's Ferry, after the original owner who began operations around 1800. Both riverbanks saw action during the Civil War. The ferry was purchased after the war by a Confederate hero named Elijah Viers White, who was also the Sheriff of Loudoun County. The present metal cable system that guides the ferry on its 1,000 foot journey was installed in the late 1870's as a replacement to a rope cable. The unique cable system is very rare now and it is said to be the last one remaining on the eastern seaboard.

Throughout its history, the ferry has changed hands several times, but remains known as White's Ferry. The current owners have had it for decades and seem committed to retaining its historical charm. The ferry boat itself, is named after General Jubal A. Early, a Confederate leader in the Civil War. In its long history, the ferry has been used to haul cargo, produce, livestock and now commuters. The current ferry boat holds up to 24 cars.

Although at one time there were many ferries on the Potomac, White's Ferry is the only one remaining. It shuttles motorists between Loudoun County in Virginia (north of Leesburg) and western Montgomery County in Dickerson, Maryland. It is the only crossing on the Potomac River between the Capital Beltway and the bridge at Point of Rocks in Frederick,  Maryland. The ferry is located at milepost 35.5 on the C&O Canal. It runs daily from 5:00 a.m. to 11:00 p.m., and cars pay $4.00 for a one-way ride or $6.00 for a roundtrip.

Of course, history alone does not tell much in the way of what you can expect as a modern day kayaker looking for a good launch site, but White's Ferry will not disappoint. For a small launch fee, you can enter the Potomac on the Maryland side at the boat ramp next to the ferry landing. Keep an eye on the ferry (which leaves every 10 minutes) if you are heading upstream. You will not have any trouble gliding over the metal cable, but don't challenge the ferry to a game of chicken, it can't move from side to side, even if the operator wanted it to—so give it a wide berth as you pass by.

You can paddle for miles both upstream and downstream, depending on the force of the current. This stretch of water is along a nice 17-mile point to point paddle from Point of Rocks to Algonkian Park, so make a roundtrip or use it as the jump-off point to a one way route.

The shoreline around White's Ferry is like much of the Potomac in the Washington area — development is nearby but not by eye, as I like to call it. You can still enjoy a nice day on the water and be removed enough from the crowds of people who live in the area to feel like you are "getting away." The Maryland side of the river follows the C&O Canal towpath and is designated parkland. The Virginia riverbank, although mostly privately owned, is also largely wooded.

Just downstream from White's Ferry is Harrison Island. The island earned its place in Civil War history as the location where Union troops crossed the river to fight a disastrous battle with the Confederates. Today the island is a protected wildlife area, so resist the temptation to get out and explore. I normally paddle to the right of the island. In low water, it can be a little tricky to pick your way along without getting beached, but most times of the year you will not have a problem.

The river at White's Ferry can have many different moods. In springtime the current can be strong, but later in the season I have taken first-timers out there to putter around in low water and get a feel for the sport. In low water, you will need to be aware of rocks both upstream and downstream. Most are easy to spot upon approach, but be careful of those lying just under the surface.

Wildlife is more plentiful on the Maryland shore, since the protected parkland provides an attractive habitat for most local critters. On a recent trip, I spotted a family of wild turkeys about a mile upstream from the ferry. A mother hen and her brood of young offspring were exploring the shoreline. Unfortunately, I startled them as I approached and she gave a signal to her kids to flee the approaching human. Feeling bad, I watched as the family scampered up the embankment to the safety of some underbrush.

There is plenty of parking on the Maryland side of White's Ferry. The area provides easy access to the C&O Canal towpath, and many bikers and hikers begin their travels from this location. There is no parking or launch area on the Virginia side of the river.

The atmosphere by White's Ferry is extremely relaxing. The ferry owners operate a convenience store with fishing supplies, groceries and a small grill. They also rent canoes during the summer. Bring a picnic and lounge around the riverbanks after your paddle, or order a burger from the grill. Be sure to check out the high water lines marked on the side of the store. It is hard to imagine the magnitude of the flood waters that engulfed the area during hurricane Agnes back in the early 1970s.

If you fish from your kayak, you will likely find the Potomac at White's Ferry to be good for smallmouth bass. Check with the Maryland Department of Natural Resources before keeping your catch, at last check this section of the Potomac was part of a designated catch-and-release zone for bass.

As with any spot on the Potomac, practice safe boating by evaluating the current water and weather conditions, and don't head out during flood conditions. The ferry operates daily unless high water or ice prevent it from doing so – but clearly, if the ferry is not running, you shouldn't be out there either!

Directions: From the Capital Beltway (Route 495) in Maryland, take Exit 39 (MD Route 190) to River Road toward Potomac. Turn left onto River Road, then right onto Partnership Road. Partnership Road turns into MD Route 107. This road merges with Whites Ferry Road. Continue until you reach the river.

White's Ferry is also reached by taking MD Route 28 west of Rockville to MD Route 107 (White's Ferry Road). From Virginia, access is from VA Route 655 off Route 15, about 4 miles northeast of Leesburg.

POINT OF ROCKS
Body of Water: Potomac River
County: Frederick
Launch Type: Ramp
Launch Fee: None
Restrooms: None
Parking: Yes

Point of Rocks is the northern most point along the C&O Canal addressed in this book.

I will share a very brief history of the canal to provide insight as to why there are so many launch points to the Potomac River alongside it.

The Chesapeake & Ohio Canal was dug around the turn of the 19th century to form a navigatible waterway for commercial trade along the Potomac River. The canal (called the C&O Canal) formed an important 184.5-mile link between Cumberland, Maryland and Washington, D.C. which allowed communities and businesses along the way to trade and sell goods. The canal contained a system of locks to allow boats, heavy with cargo such as coal, to make the descent from the mountains to the tidewaters of the river. Mule teams pulled the boats along the canal by walking on the canal towpath, which is today used for hiking and biking.

The canal ran beside the Potomac River. Later the Baltimore and Ohio Railroad (B&O Railroad – like the one in Monopoly®) was built beside the canal. The coming of the speedy railroad outdated the canal and it was

closed to commercial use in the early 20th century. A series of plans for use of the space were proposed in the following decades, including one to replace the canal with a paved highway from the city to the mountains. Eventually, through the efforts of Supreme Court Justice William O. Douglas, the C&O Canal Association was formed and later, in the 1970's, the C&O Canal National Historical Park was born.

The C&O Canal National Park is now used by outdoor enthusiasts for hiking and biking along the towpath, and by paddlers who launch at various boat ramps along the river. The ramps are also used by recreational boaters and anglers. Mileposts can be found along the towpath. The locations of many of the ramps are distinguished by the milepost to which they are closest.

Point of Rocks is a small town at canal mile marker 48 in Frederick County, Maryland. It is located between Frederick, Maryland and Leesburg, Virginia and is 12 miles by towpath to Harpers Ferry, West Virginia. Point of Rocks is named for the steep river cliffs that border the Potomac at the base of Catoctin Mountain. In fact, the cliffs themselves caused a problem during construction of the canal. Since only a small sliver of land was available between the river and the mountain, the railroad and canal builders fought over the right-of-way and held up construction of the canal for several years.

The most famous landmark in Point of Rocks is a beautiful Victorian train station that was built in the 1870's. The station is still an important stop for commuters who ride into Washington, D.C. daily by rail.

There is access to the Potomac River from both the Maryland shore and the Virginia shore next to the Route 15 bridge. Both launch areas are solid options. The public launch in Virginia is located on the first road past the bridge on Route 15 (see details in the chapter on Fairfax and Loudoun Counties). The launch on the Maryland side is located on the first turnoff on the Maryland side of the bridge (also on Route 15).

From Point of Rocks, you can paddle upstream approximately six miles to Brunswick or paddle downstream all the way to Algonkian Park (approximately 17 miles), and beyond. I prefer to paddle downstream. The current toward Brunswick can be challenging (depending on the day) but is certainly doable for most paddlers.

One of my favorite point-to-point trips in the area is from Point of Rocks to either White's Ferry or on to Algonkian Park (both are detailed in this book). It is a full day on the water, but can be very relaxing with stunning scenery – especially during peak fall foliage.

As with any river launch, be sure to check the water conditions before getting on the river. The Potomac River is a very different animal from season to season, and can be a raging beast or a kitten, depending on rainfall locally or in the mountains up river. At most times during the summer months, and especially in late summer, the water is relatively low. At those times the current is more forgiving for an upstream paddle, but more rocks will be exposed and will need to be navigated. Speaking of which, as the name suggests, there are many rocks at Point of Rocks. Do not let it keep you from paddling the area, just don't bring your brand new carbon boat on a day with low water levels.

You will more than likely be joined by small fishing boats at the launch and on the water. The Potomac is wide in this spot and has some islands (I have seen people camping on the island located just upstream from the Route 15 bridge during the summer, which looks like a fun spot) and there is plenty of room to negotiate both the rocks and other boaters. One benefit to low water levels is the clarity. I can normally see the bottom of the river around Point of Rocks, so there are few surprises waiting beneath the surface.

As you paddle downstream, you will pass by several islands between Point of Rocks and Nolands Ferry (see the following Additional Launch site section for more information on Nolands Ferry). The largest, just a few hundred yards from the bridge at Point of Rocks, is called Heaters Island. At one time the western tip of the 300-acre island housed a Piscataway fort where more than 200 Native Americans lived. Have fun picking your way around the islands and looking for wildlife. On a recent trip to the area, a large adult eagle swooped down over my kayak and landed in a tree just over the riverbank.

About mid-point between Point of Rocks and White's Ferry, the river bends near the Monocacy River Aqueduct (on your left). It is the largest aqueduct on the river and contains seven arches spanning more than 500 feet. For decades it was supported by steel beams, after sustaining damage in the flood waters of hurricane Agnes. It has since been restored and is worth a look.

Another point of interest along this stretch of the river is a whitewater kayak training facility called the Dickerson Whitewater Course (located downstream from the Monocacy River Aqueduct on the left side of the river). Many of the top whitewater boaters in the country (and many on our Olympic team) live in the Washington, D.C. area and train on the course. The course is 900 feet long and is manmade. It utilizes a section of the C&O Canal and is fueled by the Dickerson Generating Station where water diverted for power generation by the Mirant Power Plant rejoins the Potomac River. The Bethesda Center for Excellence runs the private facility.

If you continue downstream, you will come to White's Ferry and a number of additional launch sites along the river near where remains of the old canal locks still stand (such as Edwards Ferry and Sycamore Landing). You can continue on to Algonkian Regional Park on the Virginia side of the river or even turn around and paddle back upstream to Point of Rocks (depending on the current). This part of the Potomac offers endless possibilities for a day of exploration.

Directions: From Route 15 in Maryland, travel south from Frederick to the Point of Rocks Bridge. The launch is just before the bridge on the last turn-off on the left (Clay Street). There will be a sign to Route 28 east on the turn off. Once on Clay Street, make an immediate right by the sign for the C&O Canal Park & Trail onto Commerce Street. Follow Commerce Street around the corner and over the railroad tracks. Cross over the wooden bridge and follow the road to the second parking lot under the Route 15 bridge. The ramp is right under the bridge and there is limited parking.

ADDITIONAL LAUNCH SITES

NAME: CENTENNIAL PARK
Body of Water: Centennial Lake
County: Howard
Launch Type: Ramp
Launch Fee: $5.00
Restrooms: Yes
Parking: Yes

Directions: From the Capital Beltway (Route 495), take Exit 30A (Route 29 north) toward Columbia. After approximately 18 miles, take Exit 21B (Route 108 west) toward Clarksville. The park entrance is on the right (approximately one mile).

Description: Centennial Lake is a 54-acre lake in Centennial Park. Launching is available from March – November with a boating permit (available at the park). Seasonal passes are also available. The park is a total of 325 acres and has a concession stand, general store and other amenities such as pavilions and picnic areas. The lake is a very suitable location for beginning kayakers and children to paddle. Kayak instruction is offered at the park through the L.L. Bean store in Columbia. For additional information on park hours, call 410-313-4700.

NAME: ROCK CREEK REGIONAL PARK
Body of Water: Lake Needwood
County: Montgomery
Launch Type: Shoreline
Launch Fee: $5.00
Restrooms: Yes
Parking: Yes

Directions: Lake Needwood is located in Rock Creek Regional Park. From Route I-270 in Maryland, take Exit 5 (Route 189) toward Falls Road. Turn left on Great Falls Road (still Route 189). Turn right on W Jefferson Street (Route 28), then left on 1st Street (Route 28 east). Turn left onto Avery Road. Turn left on Needwood Lake Circle (15700 Needwood Lake Circle).

Description: Lake Needwood is a 75-acre lake in Rock Creek Regional Park. The boat launch area is open all year and there's a boathouse offering seasonal canoe rentals. The lake is a perfect place for beginning paddlers and children. A seasonal pass ($60.00) or daily pass ($5.00) is required to launch. Mooring sites are also available. For additional information, call the Lake Needwood Boathouse at 301-762-9500.

NAME: SENECA LANDING
Body of Water: Potomac River
County: Montgomery
Launch Type: Ramp
Launch Fee: None
Restrooms: Yes (portable)
Parking: Yes

Directions: Seneca Landing is located at milepost 22.8 on the C&O Canal towpath. From Route I-270 in Maryland, take the exit for Route 28 (west). Continue on Route 28 by Darnestown and turn left onto Seneca Road (Route 112). Follow signs for the C&O Canal Park by Seneca Creek State Park. For additional information call 301-739-4200.

Description: Launch at the end of Seneca Road onto the Potomac River (Seneca Creek State Park will be on your right as you approach the river). Paddle upstream (there are small rapids just downstream).

NAME: SYCAMORE LANDING
Body of Water: Potomac River
County: Montgomery
Launch Type: Ramp
Launch Fee: None
Restrooms: Yes (portable)
Parking: Yes

Directions: Sycamore Landing is located at milepost 27.2 on the C&O Canal. From the Capital Beltway (Route 495) in Maryland, take Exit 39A (MD Route 190) toward Potomac. Keep right on River Road. Turn left on Sycamore Landing Road. For additional information call 301-739-4200.

Description: Launch on the Potomac River across from the Van Deventer Island. Paddle across the river and around the island, or up or downstream (if you paddle downstream, be aware that there are rapids past Seneca

Landing). The launch is near a managed hunting area, so don't be surprised to hear gun-fire in the fall during hunting season.

NAME: EDWARDS FERRY
Body of Water: Potomac River
County: Montgomery
Launch Type: Ramp
Launch Fee: None
Restrooms: Yes (portable)
Parking: Yes

Directions: Edwards Ferry is located at milepost 30.8 on the C&O Canal (4.5 miles from Poolesville). From Route I-270 north in Maryland, take Exit 6B (Route 28 west) toward Darnestown. Keep left at Key West Avenue and then right at Darnestown Road and left onto Whites Ferry Road. Whites Ferry Road turns into Fisher Avenue. Turn left onto Westerly Avenue. Turn right on West Willard Road and then make an immediate left onto Westerly Road. Turn left on Edwards Ferry Road and follow it to the end. For additional information call 301-739-4200.

Description: In the early 1800s, Edwards Ferry was an important link between Maryland and Virginia on the Potomac River. Now it is a boat launch and recreation area. Drive over the canal and park in the lot between the C&O Canal and the Potomac River. The remains of a country store are alongside the road as you drive in. There is a cement ramp to launch onto the Potomac. Paddle up or downstream exploring each shoreline.

NAME: MONOCACY AQUEDUCT
Body of Water: Potomac River
County: Montgomery
Launch Type: Ramp
Launch Fee: None
Restrooms: Yes (portable)
Parking: Yes

Directions: The Monocacy Aqueduct boat launch is located at milepost 42.2 on the C&O Canal. Take Route I-270 north to Route 28. Follow Route 28 west/north to the town of Dickerson. Pass through Dickerson and continue west. Once you pass Dickerson look for signs for the C&O Canal - Mouth of the Monocacy Park Entrance (Mouth of Monocacy Road). Turn left (south) and follow the road into the Park (Note: when the road splits, follow the signs to the boat ramp).

Description: The Monocacy Aqueduct is an impressive seven-arched structure built of local quartz sandstone around 1830. It is one of 11 aqueducts built along the C&O Canal to convey the canal over rivers flowing into the Potomac. The Monocacy Aqueduct is more than 500 feet long. Launch on the Potomac River at the mouth of the Monocacy River. Explore parts of the Monocacy or head up or downstream on the Potomac River. For additional information call 301-739-4200.

NAME: NOLANDS FERRY
Body of Water: Potomac River
County: Frederick
Launch Type: Ramp
Launch Fee: None
Restrooms: Yes (portable)
Parking: Yes

Directions: The Nolands Ferry boat launch is located at milepost 44.6 on the C&O Canal. Follow Route I-270 north to Route 28 then Route 28 west/north to the town of Dickerson. Pass through Dickerson and continue west toward Tuscarora. When the road splits, turn left to stay on Route 28 but then at the next split, continue straight on Nolands Road, leaving Route 28 (28 continues to the right).

Description: Nolands Ferry provides good access to the Potomac River along the C&O Canal towpath. Across the river from the launch is Nolands Island. You can paddle around the island or up or downstream. For additional information call 301-739-4200.

NAME: *CUNNINGHAM FALLS STATE PARK*
Body of Water: Hunting Creek Lake
County: Frederick
Launch Type: Ramp
Launch Fee: $3.00 in state, $4.00 out of state
Restrooms: Yes
Parking: Yes

Directions: From I-270 north, take Route 15 north to Thurmont. Take Route 77 west (approximately 4 miles) and turn left on Catoctin Hollow Road. The boat ramp is located off Catoctin Hollow Road.

Description: Hunting Creek Lake is a small (44-acre) but scenic lake in Cunningham Falls State Park. Located in the Catoctin Mountains, the tree-lined lake and fresh air are worth a trip. No gasoline powered boats are allowed on the lake, which makes it especially nice for beginning paddlers and children. For additional information call 301-271-7574.

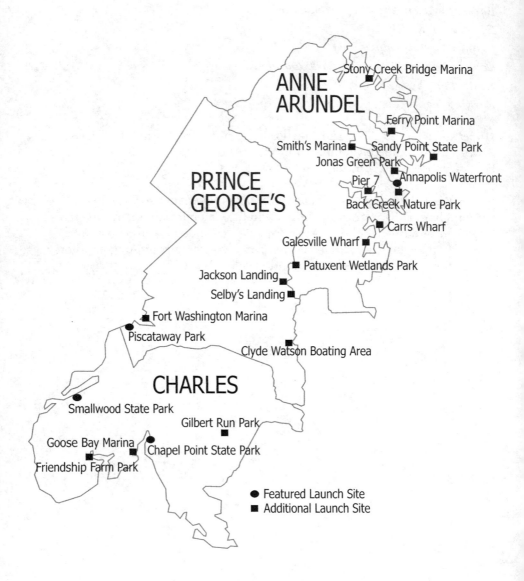

ANNE
ARUNDEL

Stony Creek Bridge Marina

Ferry Point Marina

PRINCE
GEORGE'S

Smith's Marina   Sandy Point State Park

Jonas Green Park

Pier 7   Annapolis Waterfront

Back Creek Nature Park

Carrs Wharf

Galesville Wharf

Patuxent Wetlands Park

Jackson Landing

Selby's Landing

Fort Washington Marina

Piscataway Park

Clyde Watson Boating Area

CHARLES

Smallwood State Park

Gilbert Run Park

Goose Bay Marina

Chapel Point State Park

Friendship Farm Park

● Featured Launch Site
■ Additional Launch Site

CHAPTER 4

ANNE ARUNDEL, CHARLES AND PRINCE GEORGE'S COUNTIES

ANNAPOLIS WATERFRONT
Body of Water: Spa Creek
County: Anne Arundel
Launch Type: Ramp
Launch Fee: $5.00 City Residents; $10.00 Non-city Residents
Restrooms: Yes
Parking: Yes

Several things come to mind when someone mentions Annapolis to me: sailing, the Naval Academy and eating crabs. Although white sails, white dress uniforms and plenty of scrumptious seafood are permanent features on the beautiful waterfront, if you take a closer look at the surrounding waterways, you will see kayaks slipping between sailboats and luxury cruising vessels.

Spa Creek is my choice as a jump-off point to the Annapolis area. Public launch sites are surprisingly sparse in this water-lover's paradise, but Truxtun Park is a good option. The park provides access to Spa Creek and the Annapolis waterfront and is in close proximity to the Severn River.

If you need to rent a kayak or purchase any gear, visit Annapolis Canoe and Kayak (formerly Springriver Corporation) on Third Street. They are a personal favorite of mine. Their staff is friendly and knowledgeable and they offer their customers access to their convenient dock on Spa Creek, although parking is somewhat limited.

Much of the shoreline on Spa Creek is privately owned and the vast majority is developed. I enjoy kayaking past the nicely-kept properties, and ogling the beautiful homes along the shoreline. Most of the residents have private docks but there are a few places for the general public to stop and take a break.

Paddling down Spa Creek and by the Annapolis City Dock is a different sight-seeing trip from any other location described in this book. The harbor is packed with marinas, but unlike the vast harbor in Baltimore, Annapolis is smaller and has an intimate feel. Okay, you may wonder how paddling up to a luxury sailing yacht that carries deck furniture that costs more than your boat can feel comfortable, let alone intimate, but it is the people on board (not all, but most) that give Annapolis its own fun vibe.

I have found most of the sailing crowd in Annapolis to be welcoming to kayakers and sometimes even genuinely interested in kayaks. I have had numerous friendly exchanges with people onboard massive vessels who simply wanted to know how stable kayaks are, where I learned to paddle, and if "older" people can kayak.

Be cautious when paddling into the harbor. Although the boaters may be nice, that will not stop them from running you over if they don't see you. Be extremely careful and wear bright clothing.

The colonial style waterfront is thick with restaurants, bars and shops, but the sailing and Naval Academy patrons give the area a patriotic, yet almost tropical feel. You will not have trouble identifying the famous "Ego Alley" where for decades boaters have cruised by to show off their pride and joy.

Continue out of the harbor (towards the left) and into the mouth of the Severn River. Looking right you can see out into the Chesapeake Bay and in the summer the horizon will be brimming with sails. Be alert exiting Spa Creek. The mouth of the Severn is often quite busy and wavy, with boat traffic coming off the Chesapeake up the river and into the harbor. The Naval Academy will be to your left if you head up the Severn. There is a large seawall around the compound which throws the boat wakes back at you when you paddle by. Sometimes there are nice rollers that can be fun to surf on, but when it is really busy, you will encounter more of a washing machine effect.

You could spend hours or a full day exploring the creeks that run into the Severn. I usually explore along the left shoreline instead of crossing the river. The first creek you will come to (between the grounds of the Academy) is College Creek. Paddle up past St. John's College and explore the backwater. The creek offers a nice sheltered paddle after the open Severn, and is less developed than neighboring Spa Creek.

Paddling out into the Severn again, you can continue upstream (northwest) under the Baltimore Annapolis Boulevard Bridge (Route 450), around Wardour Bluffs, and into Weems Creek. It is roughly three miles from Truxtun Park to the Route 450 bridge, so depending on how long you want to paddle, you can turn around or continue up the river to Luce Creek, Whitehurst Lake, or Saltworks Creek or even further up to Round Bay and Little Round Bay (which are roughly another five miles from the Route 450 bridge).

No matter how long you paddle, be prepared for changing tide, wind and weather conditions. Your trip up the Severn will most likely be different than your trip back down. Also be on the lookout for the Academy's crew team – they move like lightening through the water.

After a morning, afternoon or day of paddling, be sure to save time for a meal near the waterfront. Buddy's Crabs and Ribs (100 Main Street) is a great bet for some delicious Maryland crabcakes, and any night on the town should include a stop at The Rams Head Tavern (33 West Street) to share a bucket of beer with your paddling buddies.

Directions: From Route 50 east in Maryland, take Route 665 east (Aris T. Allen Blvd/Forst Drive exit) for approximately 4 miles. Turn left on Hilltop Lane. After approximately 1 mile, turn left on Primrose Road. Stay left at the fork and continue on Park Road to Truxtun Park. The park is open from dawn until dusk. For more information, contact the Recreation Department in Annapolis at 410-263-7958.

CHAPEL POINT STATE PARK
Body of Water: Port Tobacco River
County: Charles
Launch Type: Beach
Launch Fee: None
Restrooms: Yes (portable)
Parking: Yes

There's nothing like the first springtime paddle – the first nice day that happens to fall on a weekend – a day when you can trade rubber boots for sport sandals and enjoy time on the water. It was such a day that I discovered the Port Tobacco River in southern Charles County, Maryland.

I had read a little about Chapel Point State Park on the Internet, but did not know much about it other than it is a 600-acre undeveloped multi-use park. Curious to explore a potential new kayaking spot (well, new to me), I followed directions on the park web site and drove south from La Plata on Route 301.

After turning down Chapel Point Road, I drove right past the park entrance (once again!) although I was looking pretty carefully for the park sign. After turning around and trying again, I saw the big brown sign. It is fairly large, but sits just after a blind curve in the road, and only faces one direction (the wrong direction from the way I was traveling), so it really is easy to miss. Instead of looking for the park sign, look for the street sign for the road to the park, Pisces Road, it's in the middle of an open field with a rutted pea-gravel road running through it.

Pisces Road runs into the woods and down to the river. There is no boat ramp or dock, but there is a very nice ribbon of beach with a gradual decent into the water – the perfect place to launch a kayak. You will also find a decent sized sand parking area with a portable toilet. You can drive right up to the beach to unload your boat. It is free to park and free to launch.

The beach is very nice for walking during low tide. When I pulled in, a man and his small daughter were strolling by looking for shells, enjoying the beautiful spring morning together. Anchored just off shore was a small flotilla of six Sundancer® luxury powerboats from Occoquan. They were rafted up and looked like they had spent the night. It was only April, so that gives you an idea of how crowded it can get during the summer.

The beach at the park is located in a protected bay, but the water is shallow so it doesn't take much wind to create small rolling waves that break on the beach (especially at low tide). At high tide, much of the beach is covered in water, making launching and landing trickier.

The Port Tobacco River is a tributary of the Potomac River. Judging by the number of people stationed down the beach with their fishing lines out, and their apparent success rate, it seems that the fishing is excellent. A Maryland Bay Sport Tidal License is required if you are planning to try your luck.

The park is also a managed fowl hunting area, so paddle on a Sunday during hunting season (the one day of the week when hunting is not allowed) and you can enjoy viewing many different species of ducks and other birds. I have seen common golden eye ducks as well as mallards there, and several other duck species I have not been able to identify.

I was not on the water more than 30 seconds when I heard the distinct call of an osprey. Soon after, I heard another and then another. It was nesting time and there were more osprey in the trees along the shoreline than I have ever seen in one place.

I recommend paddling to the right after launching, and rounding the small peninsula that forms the outer edge of the bay. On the backside of the peninsula is the perfect wildlife habitat. Two pairs of bald eagles soared overhead, and a small otter swam out in front of my boat before realizing I was there and heading quickly for shore.

Following the main shoreline, you'll pass a mixture of private homes (some grand, some not so grand), piers and mud flats. There are also some wild marsh areas that are good for finding wildlife.

The Port Tobacco River is not a "forget where you are" wildlife experience, since plenty of boats (including police patrol boats) pass by frequently, but I was very impressed by the amount of wildlife I saw. A small aerobatics plane flew overhead at one point, and I found out later from a pilot friend that there is a school nearby where aerobatics pilots come to practice.

Depending on the wind and weather, you can paddle to the source of the river in the marsh at Port Tobacco Creek. You will recognize it by the marina and RV Park there.

If you paddle to the left from the beach launch at Chapel Point State Park, you can practice some nice open water paddling as the river meets the Potomac approximately two miles downstream. You can even view the Route 301 bridge in the distance, which spans between Virginia and Maryland another seven miles down the Potomac River.

Directions: Chapel Point State Park is located five miles south of La Plata. From the Route 6 and 301 intersection, take Route 301 south to Chapel Point Road. The park is located off Chapel Point Road (on Pisces Road), approximately 2.3 miles away.

Chapel Point State Park has a paddle-in campsite that is available all year by permit. Call 301-743-7613 for details.

SMALLWOOD STATE PARK
Body of Water: Mattawoman Creek
County: Charles
Launch Facilities: Ramp
Launch Fee: $10.00
Restrooms: Yes
Parking: Yes

I discovered Smallwood State Park by accident. My husband and a group of friends entered a well- known local triathlon back in 2000, called the "Spud Triathlon" (named after the somewhat eccentric race director's deceased cat). At the time I couldn't swim freestyle, and I was sad at the prospect of sitting on the sidelines. After exchanging a few emails with the event organizer, I decided to volunteer as kayak support during the swim leg of the race to make myself useful.

The day of the race was windy. We arrived at Smallwood State Park around 6:00 a.m. and followed the line of cars into the park. I dropped off my husband and all his gear in the race transition area and looked around for the race director. Spotting several other kayaks in the distance, I drove over to the launch area at Sweden Point Marina. The marina is a full service facility with a boathouse, bathrooms and even a small store.

Small waves were rolling onto the boat ramp and a light mist made the June morning damp and chilly. I brought the most stable of our boats, my dependable low-performance Wilderness Systems Seacret, affectionately named "Mr. Blue" for its rich blue color. Somewhat of an antique now, I knew the boat could withstand wind, rain and the scrambling hands of nervous swimmers who needed assistance during the race.

Another kayaker loudly commented how glad he was that he was kayaking and not swimming in the race. I half heartedly agreed as I struggled to pull the 60 pound boat off my car annoyed that the issuer of this comment, who showed off Herculean biceps under his inappropriately small t-shirt, failed to offer a hand as I slipped under the weight of the boat and landed in the gravel underneath it. Well, at least I got it off the car. I quickly brushed the dirt off my rear end, grabbed my gear and dragged Mr. Blue down to the water.

Smallwood was the home of a Revolutionary War General named William Smallwood who was the highest ranked officer from Maryland in the war. He was also the fourth governor of Maryland (elected in 1785). Smallwood's house, called Smallwood's Retreat, is now open to the public. The 628-acre park is located on Mattawoman Creek, a tributary of the Potomac River. The park also offers nature trails, a picnic/pavilion area, camping, a recycled tire playground and the grave of General Smallwood. Bass fishing tournaments are held regularly at the park.

The boat ramp sits on a rounded piece of land that juts out into the creek. To the left of the ramp is a large marshy area that includes a footbridge – a prime area for watching shorebirds and other wildlife. The swim for the race was held around the corner (to the right) though, past the marina's boat slips in a relatively protected area of the creek. The land formed a natural windbreaker and as I paddled out I was surprised at how calm the water was where the swimmers were warming up. As I made my way around the swim buoys, which stretched a half mile out from shore, I looked around the area. It was 45 minutes before the scheduled race start, so I took the opportunity to warm up and explore a little.

The Mattawoman Creek was downright enchanting in the early morning mist. It actually looked like a scene from a fantasy movie. Fog blanketed the water and curled up along the shore to expose clusters of bending tree limbs and branches that stretched down into the water. Paddling close to shore, I noticed a fair amount of submerged vegetation (usually fine for kayaking, but a little above my threshold for comfort while swimming as I found out the following year as a race participant). Aquatic plants are not uncommon in the Potomac tributaries, but in some spots I had to work to use my paddle. Within 100 yards from shore, the plants thinned and I felt a slight current.

It is a one mile paddle from Smallwood State Park to the Potomac River. On numerous return trips to the park, I have explored the wooded shoreline and crept through the lily pads in the marsh area looking for Heron and other birds. Boat traffic is quite heavy in the summertime. In prime time (July and August) I recommend paddling very early to avoid long lines to the boat ramp.

There is an area of the marina known as "Grinder's Wharf," which was used at one time to ship bricks from one of the region's major brick manufacturers to wholesalers. There is a natural deep water channel in the creek that led to the wharf (which is now just an area of old pilings). In the middle of the 1800's, the wharf was also used by the Washington Steamship Lines as a stop to pick up water on their route from the Potomac to the Chesapeake Bay. The marina was renovated in 2004 and 50 boat slips are now available for seasonal rentals.

The announcer's voice boomed over the intercom, and I quickly returned to my self proclaimed post by the first buoy. I was a little nervous about performing my lifesaving duties but remembered the few words of advice from the race director, "we need one boat within 100 yards of the starting line – that's about the point where people realize they can't swim in open water." I was ready. A quick glance behind me confirmed my suspicion that my Herculean gentleman friend was paddling up beside me. "Shouldn't you spread out some?" he shouted excitedly at me as he bumped Mr. Blue hard with the bow of his boat.

"Yes, you should paddle out to the turn-around buoy and count swimmers as they pass to make sure everyone is there." He nodded in agreement and quickly turned his boat around. I smiled to myself as 500 swimmers, all dressed in identical black wetsuits, goggles and swim caps waded into the water.

Directions: From the Capital Beltway (Route 495) in Maryland, take the exit for Indian Head Highway (210 south). Turn left (east) on Route 225 to Route 224. At the light, turn right onto 224 (south). The park entrance is three miles up on the right.

PISCATAWAY PARK
Body of Water: Potomac River/Piscataway Creek
County: Charles/Prince George's
Launch Facilities: Ramp
Launch Fee: None
Restrooms: None
Parking: Yes

"Let's go somewhere different" I said, standing in my driveway with my husband Pete and friend Andy, staring at the three kayaks on top of our Toyota 4Runner. It was 7:30 a.m. on the first day of October, and the sun was already out in full force. We had decided when to go kayaking, but not where to go. So there we were, thumbing through the *Maryland Delaware Atlas & Gazetteer*, trying to make a decision.

"We haven't been to Piscataway Park in a while," said Pete. "It is easy to get to and the Potomac should be pretty calm today since there is no wind and we haven't had rain in weeks." Andy agreed. He had recently paddled in Piscataway Creek while trying out a new boat at Atlantic Kayak (who has a facility right on the creek by Fort Washington

Park), and had recommended on several occasions that we go back to the area to explore more.

The decision was made. We took the Capital Beltway (Route 495) across the Woodrow Wilson Bridge to Route 210 in Maryland and turned down Marshall Hall Road (in Charles County) toward the river.

It was a Saturday morning, and when we arrived at the Marshall Hall boat ramp, the park was nearly deserted. Piscataway Park covers six miles and 5,000 acres from Marshall Hall to Piscataway Creek on the Potomac River. My first order of business was to take care of business, and I looked around for a bathroom. At the far end of the park I spotted a portable toilet. Not my first choice, but clearly my only one. I sprinted over as Pete and Andy took our boats off the car and pulled gear out of the hatch.

My first mistake was to open the fiberglass door. The waist-high weeds I had to scramble through on approach and the stench coming through the cracked door should have been a sign. As I reached for the handle, I heard a cry from a hundred yards away. "I wouldn't do that!" resonated in my ear drums before it reached my brain. As I opened the door I immediately regretted it and jumped back a few feet as the door slammed shut. A friendly golden retriever ran full throttle into the back of my leg as his owner said, "I tried to warn you" and laughed. She confirmed my suspicion that there were no other facilities and after throwing a slobbery tennis ball for her companion, I headed for some nearby woods.

The area around the ramp was somewhat littered, which was a shame because it distracted from the otherwise nice launch facility. There was no fee to launch, and no other amenities. There was plenty of parking, however, and we were on the water within minutes.

The launch is on a wide section of the Potomac River. The Maryland side of the river is mostly parkland, but the Virginia side is thickly developed with the exception of the grounds surrounding Mount Vernon, home of George Washington. The Maryland shore remains protected as it has for years, when restrictions were put in place to preserve the view from Mount Vernon.

The water was calm, but remembering a prior paddle in the area when the winds kicked-up around noon, we packed our spray skirts and started paddling up river. Piscataway Park stretches along the Potomac and into Piscataway Creek, which is just three miles from the launch at Marshall Hall. Many boats pass through this area of the river, but they mostly stay toward the middle of the river in the boat channel.

As we rounded the bend into Piscataway Creek, a large eagle swooped down over our heads and landed on a log near the edge of the water. After a closer look, we realized he had a fish in his talons and was preparing to eat his catch. Within moments, however, a hawk dropped onto the eagle's head, challenging him for his meal. The eagle dropped the fish and flew away.

Piscataway Creek is a protected inlet off the Potomac River. We paddled by the Fort Washington Marina and an adjacent kayak outfitter called Atlantic Kayak. Atlantic Kayak has an impressive stock of boats for sale and rent at their facility, and offers tours of the area.

Boat traffic was very limited in the creek, especially when compared to that on the Potomac. Across from Atlantic Kayak is a wonderful natural area with aquatic plants and a thriving waterfowl population. We enjoyed a serene paddle through the creek, stopping often to explore the shoreline and talk to other kayakers paddling out from the outfitter.

An osprey flew by as we turned to head back out of the creek. Entering the Potomac once again, we decided to cross the river and take a better look at Mount Vernon. Washington's home is clearly visible from this section of the Potomac, but we felt that crossing the busy channel would give us a better vantage point. The Woodrow Wilson Bridge is plainly visible upstream and behind it in the distance we could see the shape of the Washington Monument and the U.S. Capitol Building.

We fumbled for our spray skirts as a number of cruising ships and private boats sent large wakes rolling our way. The largest boat headed into Mount Vernon's dock. This particular ship drew an enormous, slow wake and we turned our bows in the direction of the wave and waited for it to roll underneath us, lifting our three little boats out of the water and then plopping us back down again on the other side.

Pulling up to the grounds of Mount Vernon, we drew almost as many looks from tourists on the dock as did the house itself. After taking a few pictures, we headed back across the river and back to our launch site. As with prior trips to Piscataway, the winds started to pick-up as the morning turned to afternoon. We dodged boat wakes and whitecaps as we passed through the channel, and over to the Maryland shore. We then crept back downstream using the land as a wind block until we reached the boat ramp.

While the paddling from Piscataway Park at Marshall Hall is diverse and delightful, pickings are slim for a nice place for an after paddle lunch. We settled on a sure standby of Subway® sandwiches from a nearby strip mall before heading home.

Directions: From the Capital Beltway (Route 495) in Maryland, take Exit 3 to Route 210 south. Continue on Route 210 just into Charles County. Turn right onto Marshall Hall Road (Route 227) and follow to the boat launch.

ADDITIONAL LAUNCH SITES

NAME: **STONY CREEK BRIDGE MARINA**
Body of Water: **Stony Creek**
County: **Anne Arundel**
Launch Type: **Ramp**
Launch Fee: **$15.00 weekdays & $25.00 on weekends**
Restrooms: **Yes**
Parking: **Yes**

Directions: From the Baltimore Beltway (Route 695), take Exit 1 toward Route 173 and turn right on Quarantine Road. Turn left on Hawkins Point Road (Route 173 south). Before going over the drawbridge, turn right on Greenland Beach Road. Follow to the marina.

Description: Launch on Stony Creek to explore Stony Creek and Nabbs Creek. The marina is close to the Patapsco River in a very congested area, so be aware of heavy boat traffic during the season. You can paddle around Stony Point (to the right as you enter the Patapsco River) into Rock Creek and by Fort Smallwood Park (although there are no designated landing areas in the park). For more information on the marina, call 410-255-5566.

NAME: FERRY POINT MARINA
Body of Water: Magothy River
County: Anne Arundel
Launch Type: Ramp
Launch Fee: $20.00
Restrooms: Yes
Parking: Yes

Directions: From Route 50 east in Maryland, take Exit 27 for Ritchie Highway (Route 2). Turn right onto College Parkway. Turn left onto Jones Station Road and then left again onto Mago Vista Road. Turn left onto Match Point Drive then left on River Road. Turn right on Mill Creek Road and follow to the marina (700 Mill Creek Road).

Description: Launch on the Magothy River and explore the many tributaries including Mill Creek, Dividing Creek and Cypress Creeks. There is also access to the Chesapeake Bay. Call 410-544-6368 for additional details.

NAME: SANDY POINT STATE PARK
Body of Water: Magothy River/Chesapeake Bay
County: Anne Arundel
Launch Type: Ramp and Beach
Launch Fee: $5.00 in-state, $6.00 out of state for parking, no additional
   launch fee
Restrooms: Yes
Parking: Yes

Directions: Sandy Point State Park is located directly off Route 50 just before the William Preston Lane Jr. Memorial Bridge (a.k.a. "The Bay Bridge"). From Route 50, turn left onto Bay Head Road and follow it to the park entrance.

Description: Sandy Point State Park is a 786-acre park located next to the Chesapeake Bay Bridge. There are 22 boat ramps and a beach area designated as a launch site for small watercraft such as kayaks. Paddle along the shoreline or out into the bay, but be very careful of strong currents and boat traffic as you head away from shore. The Chesapeake Bay is four miles across at this location and only experienced kayakers should venture a crossing.

NAME: JONAS GREEN PARK
Body of Water: Severn River
County: Anne Arundel
Launch Type: Beach
Launch Fee: None
Restrooms: Yes (portable)
Parking: Yes

Directions: From Route 695 in Maryland, take Route 97 south to Route 50 east. Take Exit 27A to Ritchie Highway (Route 450) and follow Route 450 towards the Naval Academy. Before crossing the Naval Academy Bridge, turn left at the light onto Route 648 and then make an immediate right to reach Jonas Green Park.

Description: Launch on the Severn River with access to many tributaries, including Spa Creek and Weems Creek. You can also paddle into the Chesapeake Bay. Be aware of strong currents, boat traffic and waves if crossing the river.

NAME: SMITH'S MARINA
Body of Water: Severn River
County: Anne Arundel
Launch Type: Ramp
Launch Fee: 15.00
Restrooms: Yes
Parking: Yes

Directions: From Route I-95 north in Maryland, take Exit 38A (Route 32) east toward Fort Meade. Route 32 becomes Route I-97 south. Take Exit 5 to Generals Highway (Route 178) south toward Crownsville. Turn left on Herald Harbor Road and follow to the end. Turn left on River Road and then take your first right onto Ridgeley Road. Follow to the marina.

Description: Launch from the marina into Little Round Bay on the Severn River. Paddle upstream to explore many coves and creeks, or downstream toward Annapolis. The ramp is closed December through mid-May. Call 410-923-3444 for additional information.

NAME: BACK CREEK NATURE PARK
Body of Water: Back Creek
County: Anne Arundel
Launch Type: Grass
Launch Fee: None
Restrooms: Yes (seasonal)
Parking: Yes (limited)

Directions: From Route I-95 in Maryland, take Exit 19A for Route 50 east.
Take Exit 22 for Route 665 south (Aris T. Allen Blvd). The road turns into
Forest Drive and then merges with Bay Ridge Road. Turn left on Edgewood
Road. The park will be on your left.

Description: Back Creek Nature Park is an Annapolis city park. Car-top
launching is available onto Back Creek, with access to the Severn River,
Chesapeake Bay and Spa Creek. There's an Osprey Nature Center in the
park. For more information call 410-263-7958.

NAME: PIER 7
Body of Water: South River
County: Anne Arundel
Launch Type: Ramp and Beach
Launch Fee: $10.00
Restrooms: Yes
Parking: Yes

Directions: From US-50, take Exit 22 for Route 665 south (Aris T. Allen
Blvd). Turn right on Solomons Island Road toward Edgewater (Route 2).
Turn left onto Route 553 (Old South River Road) and follow to Pier 7.

Description: Launch either from the beach or ramp onto the South River.
There's easy access to many creeks such as Gingerville Creek, Beards Creek,
Broad Creek, Church Creek and Crab Creek. For more information call 410-
956-2288. The launch area is open all year.

NAME: CARRS WHARF
Body of Water: Rhode River
County: Anne Arundel
Launch Type: Natural Area
Launch Fee: None
Restrooms: None
Parking: Yes (limited)

Directions: From Route 50 east in Maryland, take Exit 16 (Route 424) toward Davidsonville. Turn left on Central Avenue (Route 214). Central Avenue becomes Mayo Road. Turn right onto Carrs Wharf Road and follow to the launch.

Description: Access from Carrs Wharf is on the Rhodes River. From there you can explore Whitemarsh Creek, Bear Neck Creek, Sellman Creek, Fox Creek (near Big Island), Boathouse Creek and Muddy Creek. The Wharf is open during daylight hours. For additional information call 410-222-7317.

NAME: GALESVILLE WHARF
Body of Water: West River
County: Anne Arundel
Launch Type: Natural
Launch Fee: None
Restrooms: None
Parking: Yes

Directions: From the Capital Beltway in Maryland (Route 495), take Exit 19A to Route 50 (toward Annapolis). Take Exit 16 (Route 424 south) toward Davidsonville. Route 424 becomes Birdsville Road. Turn right briefly onto Solomons Island Road (Route 2), then left onto Mill Swamp Road. Turn right on Muddy Creek Road and then left onto Galesville Road. Follow to the wharf.

Description: Launch next to the pier (there is an area worn from use). The launch is easily accessible and open all year during daylight hours. Launch onto the West River. From there you can reach the Rhode River and the Chesapeake Bay. For additional information call 410-222-7317. There are no restrooms at the site, but commercial establishments are nearby.

NAME: PATUXENT WETLANDS PARK
Body of Water: *Patuxent River*
County: Anne Arundel
Launch Type: Floating Dock / Natural area
Launch Fee: None
Restrooms: Yes (portable - in season only)
Parking: Yes

Directions: From Route 301 in Maryland, take Route 4 south to Waysons Corner and then turn left onto Mount Zion – Marlboro Road (Route 408). Follow signs to Patuxent Wetlands Park.

Description: This launch site is only accessible at high tide (at low tide it is a mud flat). The water is very shallow. Paddle left to the Patuxent River. From there you can access Jug Bay downstream. The launch is open sunrise to sunset. Call 410-222-7317 for additional information.

NAME: GOOSE BAY MARINA
Body of Water: Goose Creek
County: Charles
Launch Type: Ramp
Launch Fee: $7.00
Restrooms: Yes
Parking: Yes

Directions: From the Capital Beltway (Route 495) in Maryland, take Exit 7A towards Waldorf on Route 5. Continue on Route 5 until it merges with Route 301. Take Route 301 to Route 6 in La Plata (going South). From Route 6, turn left on Blossom Point Road. Turn left on Brentland and then right at the Goose Bay sign. Drive to the end of the road and into the marina.

Description: Goose Bay Marina is primarily a powerboat facility, but kayaks are allowed to launch there as well. Explore Goose Creek and paddle into the Port Tobacco River.

NAME: FRIENDSHIP FARM PARK AND BOAT LAUNCH
Body of Water: Nanjemoy Creek
County: Charles
Launch Type: Ramp
Launch Fee: None
Restrooms: None
Parking: Yes

Directions: From the Capital Beltway (Route 495) in Maryland, take Exit 7A towards Waldorf on Route 5. Continue on Route 5 until it merges with Route 301. Take Route 301 to Route 6 in La Plata. Take Route 6 south to Durham Church Road. Turn left on Friendship Landing and drive through Friendship Farm Park to the launch on Nanjemoy Creek.

Description: Friendship Farm Park is a very nice Charles County Park. Although the ramp can be crowded on a nice day, you can paddle miles of scenic marshes along tidal portions of the Nanjemoy Creek. In the upper reaches of the creek is a nature preserve that claims the largest great blue heron rookery on the east coast north of Florida. The creek also provides habitat for the dwarf wedge mussel. Nanjemoy Creek flows into the Potomac and the area is good for viewing bald eagles.

NAME: GILBERT RUN PARK
Body of Water: Wheatley Lake
County: Charles
Launch Type: Ramp
Launch Fee: $4.00 (parking fee)
Restrooms: Yes
Parking: Yes

Directions: From the Capital Beltway (Route 495) in Maryland, take Exit 7A towards Waldorf on Route 5. Continue on Route 5 until you reach Oliver's Shop Road. Turn right on Oliver's Shop Road. After about six miles, turn left on Charles Street (Route 6). Gilbert Run Park is located eight miles east of La Plata on Route 6 (13140 Charles Street).

Description: Gilbert Run Park offers a 60-acre freshwater lake which can be a good choice for beginning paddlers or children. There's also a Nature Center at the park. The park is open from March to November. Call 301-932-1083 for additional details.

NAME: FORT WASHINGTON MARINA
Body of Water: Piscataway Creek
County: Prince George's
Launch Type: Ramp
Launch Fee: $5.00
Restrooms: Yes
Parking: Yes

Directions: From the Capital Beltway (Route 495) in Maryland, take Exit 2A toward Indian Head on Route 210. Turn right onto Fort Washington Road. Turn left onto Lenfant Drive then turn right onto Kings Lane. Turn left onto Reid Lane and then turn left onto Warburton Drive. Turn right onto King Charles Terrace (13600 King Charles Terrace).

Description: Fort Washington Marina is located on Piscataway Creek. Launch at the marina and explore the creek or paddle into the Potomac River. The marina is open all year. Call 301-292-7700 for additional information.

NAME: JACKSON LANDING (PATUXENT RIVER PARK)
Body of Water: Patuxent River
County: Prince George's
Launch Type: Dock
Launch Fee: $5.00 (county residents) $10.00 (non-county residents)
Restrooms: Yes (portable)
Parking: Yes

Directions: From the Capital Beltway (Route 495) in Maryland, take Exit 11A (Route 4) east to Route 301 south. Turn left on Croom Road (Route 382) and follow to Croom Airport Road. Turn left on Croom Airport Road and follow for two miles to the park entrance. To obtain a park permit, continue 1.7 miles to the park office. To continue on to the launch, follow the park road past the Visitors Center to the bottom of the hill.

Description: Jackson Landing is located in Patuxent River Park on the Patuxent River. A park permit is required for launching (must be displayed on your vehicle). Permits can be purchased at the park headquarters in the Jug Bay Natural Area (yearly passes are available). Explore the natural shoreline of this remote and beautiful area of the Patuxent River. The park has more than 6,000 acres and the Jug Bay Natural area is an important freshwater estuary in the Chesapeake Bay region. Call 301-627-6074 for additional details.

NAME: SELBY'S LANDING (PATUXENT RIVER PARK)
Body of Water: Patuxent River
County: Prince George's
Launch Type: Beach
Launch Fee: $5.00 (county residents) $10.00 (non-county residents)
Restrooms: Yes (portable)
Parking: Yes

Directions: From the Capital Beltway (Route 495) in Maryland, take Exit 11A (Route 4) east to Route 301 south. Turn left on Croom Road (Route 382 south) and follow to Croom Airport Road. Turn left on Croom Airport Road and follow for two miles to the park entrance. To obtain a park permit, continue 1.7 miles to the park office. To go to the launch, follow Croom Road (past the park entrance) until it dead ends. Turn left and follow the road to the designated area.

Description: Selby's Landing is another wonderful launch site located in the Patuxent River Park on the Patuxent River. A park permit is required for launching (must be displayed on your vehicle). Permits can be purchased at the park headquarters in the Jug Bay Natural Area (yearly passes are available). Launch on the beach to the right of the ramp and explore the natural shoreline of this area of the Patuxent River. Call 301-627-6074 for additional details.

NAME: CLYDE WATSON BOATING AREA (PATUXENT RIVER PARK)
Body of Water: Patuxent River
County: Prince George's
Launch Type: Ramp
Launch Fee: $5.00 (county residents) $10.00 (non-county residents)
Restrooms: Yes
Parking: Yes

Directions: From the Capital Beltway (Route 495) in Maryland, take Exit 11A (Route 4) east to Route 301 south. Turn left on Croom Road (Route 382 south). Go approximately 12 miles and turn left onto Magruder's Ferry Road. Follow to the launch.

To obtain a park permit, turn left on Croom Airport Road from Croom Road and follow to the Patuxent River Park entrance. Continue 1.7 miles to the park office.

Description: Clyde Watson Boating Area provides additional access to the Patuxent River in southern Prince George's County. There is a boat ramp and small beach area with picnic tables. Limited parking is available. A park permit is required for launching (must be displayed on your vehicle). Permits can be purchased at the park headquarters in the Jug Bay Natural Area (yearly passes are available). Call 301-627-6074 for additional details.

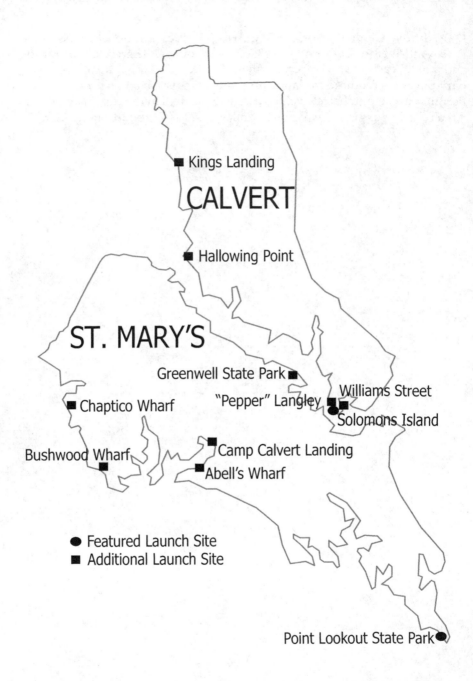

Kings Landing

CALVERT

Hallowing Point

ST. MARY'S

Greenwell State Park

Williams Street

"Pepper" Langley

Solomons Island

Chaptico Wharf

Camp Calvert Landing

Bushwood Wharf

Abell's Wharf

● Featured Launch Site
■ Additional Launch Site

Point Lookout State Park

CALVERT AND ST. MARY'S COUNTIES

SOLOMONS ISLAND
Body of Water: Patuxent River/Chesapeake Bay
County: Calvert
Launch Type: Beach
Launch Fee: None
Restrooms: Yes
Parking: Yes

"What's not to like about Solomons Island?" Was the comment I received from my enthusiastic cousin as he smiled behind a tall Mai Tai at the Tiki Bar on Charles Street. I had to agree. I came to the island as a child with my parents to watch model boat races and returned during my college years to discover sailing and the island's famous Tiki Bar. Now, years later (I won't say how many!), I return

time and again to kayak around its nooks and crannies, and to soak in a bit of the coastal atmosphere.

I wouldn't really call Solomons Island a beach setting, and I wouldn't really put it in the same category as the glamorous nautical city of Annapolis, but Solomons Island is definitely a sailor's (and now kayaker's) paradise. It is located on the point where the Patuxent River flows into the Chesapeake Bay, and has its own comfortable ambiance that I would describe as hip but with a family flare. There is one main street that loops around the point where the Patuxent and Chesapeake join, and it is lined with restaurants and shops. I find it very relaxing and easy to move around, although it can be quite crowded in the summertime.

I prefer to kayak in the off season or early in the morning to avoid the heavy boat traffic. But even on a cloudy day in June, I have found solitude while paddling off the banks of the Patuxent and the opportunity to explore uninterrupted. My favorite launch spot is adjacent to the public parking lot. If you come into town via the Governor Thomas Johnson Bridge on Route 4, turn right and head down the main strip (Solomons Island Road). The parking lot is on the right side of the road next to the turquoise Solomons Boat Rental building (you can't miss it). It is the first public parking lot across from the Catholic Church.

Park on the very northern end of the lot and step over the railroad ties behind the DO NOT THROW LITTER $1,000 FINE sign. You will find a nice beach with clean sand on the other side. There are no markers or signs indicating that it is a launch site, but the pretty little beach lends itself perfectly to launching your boat. There are public restrooms across from the gazebo by the public parking lot.

Once on the river (this is the Patuxent side of the island), you can paddle north toward the bridge or south around the tip of Solomons Island into Back Creek, or even out to the Chesapeake Bay.

The shoreline of the Patuxent River in Solomons Island is a mixture of seawall/boardwalk and piers. As you round the tip of the island, another seawall protects the island from the force of the Bay currents and waves. Rounding the point into Back Creek, you'll find a protected oasis to paddle in. Add a few palm trees and you could be on the gulf coast somewhere as the shoreline is filled with marinas, seafood restaurants and a jovial sailing crowd.

Back Creek is a good option to begin exploration of the area. It can be especially crowded, however, so pick a non-peak time to paddle to optimize the experience. The opportunities for paddling are endless, just watch for tides and currents (give the Chesapeake the respect it deserves).

If you need to rent a kayak, the local outfitter, Patuxent Adventure Center, offers a varied selection of boats and equipment, and also offers instruction and guided tours. The folks there are very helpful and friendly, and customers can even launch from a private site behind the store on Back Creek.

Solomons Island is a true gem for the Baltimore/Washington, D.C. crowd. An easy drive transports you to a relaxed vacation atmosphere with plenty of water for boaters of all varieties. There are too many great seafood restaurants to narrow down my favorite – but if you are in the mood for crabs, fish and other delights from the sea, you won't be disappointed by the selection. If you are more in the mood for a relaxing cocktail – then by all means stop by the Tiki Bar – just don't plan to drive home right afterwards!

Directions: Solomons Island is located in Solomons, Maryland. From the Capital Beltway (Route 495) take Exit 11 (Route 4) south (Pennsylvania Avenue extended) toward Upper Marlboro. Follow Route 4 approximately 55 miles (it will join Route 2 just above Prince Frederick). Traveling south on Route 4, just past the Solomons Fire and Rescue Squad, turn right at the light at Patuxent Point Parkway and follow to Asbury~Solomons Island.

POINT LOOKOUT STATE PARK
Body of Water: Potomac River/Chesapeake Bay
County: St. Mary's
Launch Type: Ramp
Launch Fee: $6.00 Non-Maryland resident entrance fee
  $5.00 Maryland resident entrance fee
  $10.00 launch fee
Restrooms: Yes
Parking: Yes

"Are you here for the swim?" asked the friendly blond woman in the park reception booth as she looked up at the kayak on our car. We answered in the affirmative, and tried to pay the park entrance fee. She promptly returned the money, handed us a park map and said, "Have a nice day."

Feeling a little sheepish, we drove into the park. Technically, we were there for the swim, but we were not actually participating or supporting it – we were there more in a cheering capacity. My good friend Lindsey was entered in the Chesapeake Swim for the Environment – a challenging 7 ½ mile swim from the banks of the Potomac River in Virginia, to the mouth of the Chesapeake Bay at Point Lookout State Park in St. Mary's County, Maryland. My husband was providing kayak support to Lindsey, supplying food, water, encouragement and the navigation skills of his GPS system to escort her safely across the open water. My friend Andy and I were training for a 90-mile kayak race, and seized the opportunity to fit in an early morning workout while the bulk of the race occurred offshore. We then planned to cheer in Lindsey at the finish.

The trip from my home in Reston, Virginia to the park was easy given that we left at 6:00 a.m. on a Saturday. It is a bit of a hike down the Beltway to Route 4 or Route 5 (both get you where you're going in about the same amount of time), although still an easy commute for a day trip.

Our first task was to locate my boat. I figured this would be easy since it sits up pretty high on top of my husband's 4Runner (he had driven down the night before for some pre-race festivities) however there were three possible parking areas. Of course, we should have guessed that he would be parked by the boat ramp, but we first checked out the lighthouse parking area at the tip of the peninsula (the park truly is a point sticking out into the Chesapeake), and then the picnic/beach area where the race finished.

Finally, after pulling into the boat launch area, we spotted my kayak, quickly unloaded our gear and paid the $10.00 launch fee.

As I was stuffing my keys into my drybag, Andy said, "there's a snake over here, but I think it's dying." I looked at the rocks piled up along the shoreline next to the boat ramp and saw a rather thick but pleasant-looking brown snake stretched out.

"Are you sure it's not sunning itself?" I asked.

"Well, I touched its tail and it just barely moved" Andy explained. I had to agree, the snake didn't look very lively. Just then, a park ranger came by. We asked if the snake was okay. He called over a second ranger and the two stood over the snake.

"Is it a water moccasin?" I asked.

"No, we don't have those here. These will give you a nasty infection if they bite, but they aren't poisonous. Say, this is a little one," said the first ranger.

"Yeah, nothing like old Oscar," said the second.

"Who's Oscar?" I asked, shifting my kayak into the water and rolling up my paddling pants.

"He's a really old grumpy one who lives over there around the end dock," he said, pointing to a dock a few yards away. "They're pretty tame on land, but once they get in the water, they can get aggressive. Say – this one's okay – he just went into the water."

I turned as I was getting into my boat, knee deep in the water – just feet from where "the little one" slithered in for a swim. The rangers stood smiling.

I quickly dropped into my kayak and paddled away from shore, yelling to Andy over my shoulder that he could paddle out to meet me.

The boat ramp puts you on Lake Conoy, in a large protected area between the Potomac and a causeway that separates the lake from the Chesapeake. It was a beautiful calm June morning and the water was still. Sitting there waiting for Andy, I looked up into a large dead tree at the edge of the water; there sat a beautiful bald eagle. He was breathtaking. Wishing I had a more powerful camera with me, I managed to take a few pictures before he flew off.

"Well, that was worth the trip already," I said, and we turned to explore the lake.

Point Lookout is a haven for birds. I know I say that about every trip because, let's face it, we're not looking for whales or caribou in the Baltimore/Washington, D.C. area and large raptors can be about as good as it gets – but this place was loaded. There were juvenile eagles calling in their rather "girly" sounding voices (I know I will take some heat from avid birders, including my mother, but I've always been surprised at how delicate a call these large, strong birds make). There were also more blue herons than I've ever seen in one location, and numerous osprey (one of my personal favorites).

We took our time moseying around the lake, exploring its grassy shoreline, completely forgetting that we were not there to sightsee, but to get a good workout in preparation for our race. But the tranquility of the lake and the abundant wildlife made our goal hard to remember. We explored each nook and cranny of the lake for a possible outlet to the bay or the river, moving so slowly that we could get a good look at a few snapping turtle heads before they scurried underwater. Finally, after deciding that it wasn't worth slipping limbo-style under a very low bridge into the last unexplored passageway, we concluded that we needed to head toward the launch site to paddle out to the Potomac side of the park where the swimmers would soon come in.

On return trips to the park, I have enjoyed a challenging paddle through incoming waves on the Potomac side of the park, as well as more tranquil paddles on both the Potomac and the Chesapeake sides. The park offers an interesting diversity of conditions with the lake, river and bay right at your fingertips, and the park itself offers a nice atmosphere for picnicking and spending a day.

In contrast to the relaxing, serene environment found at Point Lookout today, the park has a very turbulent history. It was the site of the largest prison camp during the Civil War, holding up to 20,000 men at a time. Many prisoners froze to death at the overcrowded camp and many others perished trying to escape.

Numerous stories of past and present day ghost sightings are recorded in the park, and some believe the lighthouse (which still stands) is the most haunted site in the park. Various visitors and a team of researches reported hearing nearly two dozen different voices in the lighthouse, smelled an unexplainable rotten aroma in one particular room and saw odd visions of people dressed in period clothing. I can't say that I have ever experienced a ghostly encounter in the times I've paddled there, but the possibility of a ghost sighting certainly adds an element of excitement to an otherwise serene outing.

Directions: From the Capital Beltway (Route 495) in Maryland, take the exit for Route 4 (Pennsylvania Avenue) south to Upper Marlboro. Continue on Route 4 until you cross the Solomons Island Bridge. After the bridge, turn left at the first traffic light onto Route 235 south. Continue to Route 5 and turn left (south). Follow Route 5 to the park.

ADDITIONAL LAUNCH SITES

NAME: "PEPPER" LANGLEY FISHING PIER AND BOAT LAUNCH FACILITY
Body of Water: Patuxent River
County: Calvert
Launch Type: Ramp
Launch Fee: $5.00
Restrooms: Yes
Parking: Yes

Directions: This launch is located next to the Thomas Johnson Bridge coming into Solomons Island (across from the Calvert Marine Museum, which is worth a visit). Turn right after crossing the bridge and follow signs to the boat launch.

Description: This is a large boat launch facility that can be crowded with powerboat traffic. On the plus side, it is a full-service facility with convenient access to the Patuxent River in Solomons Island. There is a Visitors Center nearby, plenty of parking and permanent restrooms.

NAME: WILLIAMS STREET LAUNCH (SOLOMONS ISLAND)
Body of Water: Back Creek / Chesapeake Bay
County: Calvert
Launch Type: Ramp
Launch Fee: None
Restrooms: None
Parking: None

Directions: This somewhat hidden ramp is located near the end of the point on Solomons Island, next to the police station on Williams Street. There is no parking by the ramp, so look for nearby street parking.

Description: This boat ramp is a quiet, isolated launch point to Back Creek and the Chesapeake Bay on Solomons Island.

NAME: HALLOWING POINT PUBLIC BOAT RAMP
Body of Water: Patuxent River
County: Calvert
Launch Type: Ramp
Launch Fee: None
Restrooms: Yes (portable)
Parking: Yes

Directions: This ramp is located on Route 231 on the left side of the road just before the Patuxent River Bridge on the Calvert County side. Turn onto Hallowing Lane and follow past the Visitors Center to the end.

Description: This is not a fancy facility, but it provides good access to the Patuxent River from the Calvert County side of the Patuxent River Bridge. For more information call 410-535-3382.

NAME: KINGS LANDING PARK
Body of Water: Patuxent River
County: Calvert
Launch Type: Natural
Launch Fee: None
Restrooms: Yes (portable)
Parking: Yes

Directions: From the Capital Beltway (Route 495) in Maryland. Take Exit 11A (Route 4 south). Turn right on Route 262 (Lower Marlboro Road), then left on Huntingtown Road. Turn right on Kings Landing Park Road (once you see the sign for the park, continue straight to the parking area).

Description: Kings Landing is a scenic park that offers access to the Patuxent River, but you will need to carry your boat 200-300 yards from the parking area to the river. Launch next to the fishing pier. The park is open from 8:30 a.m. to 4:30 p.m. For additional details call 410-535-2661.

NAME: CHAPTICO WHARF
Body of Water: Wicomico River
County: St. Mary's
Launch Type: Ramp/Dock
Launch Fee: None
Restrooms: Yes (portable)
Parking: Yes (limited)

Directions: From the Capital Beltway (Route 495) in Maryland, take Exit 7A towards Waldorf on Route 5. Continue on Route 5 into St. Mary's County. Continue on Route 5 until you reach Route 238 (be sure to keep right on Route 5 when it meets Route 235). Turn right on Route 238 (Budds Creek Road). Follow Route 238 through Chaptico (Route 238 turns into Maddox Road in town) and turn right on Old Chaptico Wharf Road. There is a sign for the Chaptico Wharf Recreation Area.

Description: Launch on the Wicomico River (which is a state-designated scenic river) and paddle either to the right around the point into the Chaptico Bay or explore the shoreline along the river. A paddle upstream will take you to the confluence of the Zekiah Swamp Run and the Wicomico River at the Zekiah Swamp Natural Environmental Area. Look for osprey.

NAME: BUSHWOOD WHARF
Body of Water: Wicomico River
County: St. Mary's
Launch Type: Ramp
Launch Fee: None
Restrooms: Yes
Parking: Yes

Directions: From the Capital Beltway (Route 495) in Maryland, take Exit 7A towards Waldorf on Route 5. Continue on Route 5 into St. Mary's County. Continue on Route 5 until you reach Route 238. Turn right on Route 238 (Budds Creek Road). Follow Route 238 through Chaptico (Route 238 turns into Maddox Road in town). Continue on Route 238/Maddox Road and turn right on Bushwood Road. Bushwood Road joins Bushwood Wharf Road.

Description: Bushwood Wharf is located in the Robert F. Pogue Memorial Park. As the sign coming into the park will tell you, the location was a steamboat wharf until 1930 and was also occupied by Union troops during the Civil War. Launch in a small cove on the Wicomico River (which is a state-designated scenic river) near its mouth where it meets the Potomac River. Be careful of strong winds that can come off the Potomac. Look for herons and other shore birds. There is a small marina and store by the launch.

NAME: CAMP CALVERT LANDING
Body of Water: Breton Bay
County: St. Mary's
Launch Type: Beach
Launch Fee: None
Restrooms: None
Parking: Yes (very limited)

Directions: From the Capital Beltway (Route 495) in Maryland, take Exit 7A towards Waldorf on Route 5. Continue on 5 until you reach the Leonardtown area. Turn right very briefly onto Fenwick Street, before turning left onto Camp Calvert Road and follow to the water.

Description: This is a simple but scenic launch onto Breton Bay. The launch is on soft sand. There are trash receptacles but no other amenities. Breton Bay provides access to the Potomac River.

NAME: ABELL'S WHARF
Body of Water: Breton Bay
County: St. Mary's
Launch Type: Ramp/Beach
Launch Fee: None
Restrooms: Yes (portable)
Parking: Yes

Directions: From the Capital Beltway (Route 495) in Maryland, take Exit 7A towards Waldorf on Route 5. Continue on Route 5 into St. Mary's County. Follow Route 5 to Route 244. Turn right on Route 244 (Beauvue Rd). Turn right on Breton Beach Road then right again on Abell's Wharf Road. Follow to the launch.

Description: Abell's Wharf is located on a small sheltered bay on Breton Bay. It is usually an easy paddle across Breton Bay, but be aware of barges and tugboats coming and going from the sand company located right next door. You can also paddle upstream toward Camp Calvert Landing or downstream to the Potomac River. The area boasts a wealth of wildlife. Look particularly for osprey and horseshoe crabs.

NAME: GREENWELL STATE PARK
Body of Water: Patuxent River
County: St. Mary's
Launch Type: Beach
Launch Fee: $3.00 (park entrance)
Restrooms: Yes
Parking: Yes

Directions: From the Capital Beltway (Route 495) in Maryland, take Exit 7A towards Waldorf on Route 5. Continue on Route 5 into St. Mary's County. When Route 5 and Route 235 join, stay straight on Route 235. Follow Route 235 to Hollywood and turn left on Route 245 (Sotterley Road). Turn right onto Steer Horn Neck Road. Turn left at the park entrance.

Description: Walk your kayak down to the launch at the designated canoe and kayak beach. The launch is in a sheltered cove. The launch offers a nice opportunity to explore tidal wetlands around the 596-acre park. Primitive camping facilities are available by water. Call 301-373-9775 for more information.

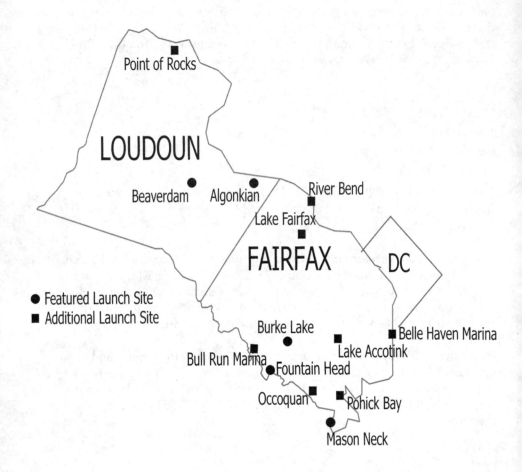

Point of Rocks

LOUDOUN

Beaverdam   Algonkian   River Bend

Lake Fairfax

FAIRFAX   DC

● Featured Launch Site
■ Additional Launch Site

Burke Lake   Belle Haven Marina

Bull Run Marina   Lake Accotink

Fountain Head

Occoquan   Pohick Bay

Mason Neck

FAIRFAX AND LOUDOUN COUNTIES

ALGONKIAN REGIONAL PARK
Body of Water: Potomac River
County: Loudoun
Launch Type: Ramp
Launch Fee: $5.00 ($35.00 annual pass)
Restrooms: Yes (near picnic shelters 1 and 2 and by the pro golf shop)
Parking: Yes

If you were not looking for it, you would probably miss Algonkian Regional Park in Sterling, Virginia. Appropriately named for the language relation shared by native American tribes in this area before the English came, I think of the park as the gateway to the Potomac of yesteryear.

Although for many years Algonkian Park stood alone "in the middle of nowhere," – as my sister described it when we first went there as children; you'll now doubt my judgment for recommending it as you approach it via a maze of housing developments and strip malls. However, once you pass the golf course and turn toward the boat ramp, you will get a glimpse of the majestic Potomac as it once flowed undisturbed.

There is something arresting about the Potomac by Algonkian. The river is wide and (usually) lazy as it winds toward the thundering hydraulics that gave Great Falls its name (don't worry, you are still a few miles upstream from the

falls at this part of the river). The shoreline is forested on both sides, and the canal towpath is just barely recognizable on the far Maryland bank as the occasional cyclist appears and then disappears again into the trees.

A large map of the river is posted next to the boat ramp along with a little box to collect launch fees. Be sure to survey the river before heading out. As with most rivers in the area, the flow varies considerably by season, and the current can be swift after heavy or prolonged rain and in the spring.

I will be honest, on a summer weekend the ramp will be packed with jet skis, so plan to go early in the day, on a weekday, or (better yet), in the spring or fall when the water is cold. If you must go during a nice summer weekend, it will not be a loss; once you clear the ramp and head upstream, it will only be a matter of minutes before you leave the congested area of the river and are soon accompanied by only the occasional fisherman or canoeist.

The paddle upstream is noticeably free of development and you'll soon forget that the area is surrounded by neighborhoods. Except for passing planes heading to or from Dulles Airport, it is also unusually silent. Several large islands divide the Virginia and Maryland banks near the park. This allows for a nice change of scenery between the paddle upstream and the trip back. I usually paddle up the left side of the islands (Virginia side) and paddle down the much wider Maryland side.

The length of your trip is at your discretion. The river flow will determine how quickly you are able to paddle upstream. In the spring, or after rain, the water can move deceivingly quickly, but normally it is slow and easy to move upstream. In the summer the water levels can be very low (especially near the Virginia banks) and you can often see down to the sandy bottom just a few inches below your seat.

The shore along the park is randomly dotted with park-owned cabins, but they can be difficult to see when the trees have leaves. They are fully equipped and are available for rent (visit www.nvrpa.org/cottages for details). Once you paddle past the park, residential homes — most which have been there for many years — are the only buildings you will see and these are few and far between.

One of my favorite things to do when the water level is reasonably low is to pack a lunch and paddle past the second big island upstream from the park (Van Deventer Island). Just after passing the island you will see a passage to the main part of the river where sandy beaches are exposed (between Van Deventer Island and Selden Island). These islands are the perfect spot for lunch or a midday nap. If the water is low, you may paddle in just a few inches of water, but when the water or wind is high, it can be a challenging padde through the current that sweeps through the passage. Although I usually do not run into anyone there, it is possible to share the islands with overnight campers. You'll feel a million miles from the city as you lounge around your "private" island in the middle of the river. When the water is low, it will only take you about an hour to paddle to this area, but when the current is strong, it can take twice as long. Of course, then the trip downstream is that much faster.

Wildlife in this area will most commonly take the form of the blue heron. They are abundant, especially when the water levels are low and they can wade far out to fish. I have also spotted several types of hawks, turkeys and even bald eagles in close proximity to the park.

As for the wildlife of the four-legged variety, deer can be seen grazing along the shore and river otters sometimes frolic in the shallows in the early morning. Turtles are also common along this route and will lie in lines atop sunken tree branches and then plunge one by one into the water when they see you approach.

Fishing near Algonkian is reportedly good. Expect to find largemouth bass, smallmouth bass, catfish, bluegill, crappie and carp. A fishing license is required.

From Algonkian Park, you can paddle downstream about a mile and a half to Seneca Breaks before the going gets rocky (there are class 1 rapids from Seneca Breaks down to River Bend Park).

Directions: To reach Algonkian Regional Park from the Beltway (I-495), take the exit for Route 7 (toward Tysons Corner) and continue west. Continue until you reach the exit for the Fairfax County Parkway and Algonkian Parkway and turn right onto Algonkian Parkway. Follow the sign to the park by turning right onto Cascades Parkway (47001 Fairway

Drive, Sterling). Follow the signs to the boat launch area. Call 703-450-2806 for additional information.

BEAVERDAM CREEK RESERVOIR
Body of Water: Beaverdam Creek Reservoir
County: Loudoun
Launch Type: Dirt Landing
Launch Fee: None
Restrooms: None
Parking: Yes

Although I live within 20 miles of Beaverdam Creek Reservoir in Loudoun County, Virginia, I had never even heard of it until a few years ago when some triathlete friends stopped showing up for our weekend swims at a local lake. Over breakfast one morning, I asked them why they were no longer swimming with us. They looked kind of sheepish and explained, "we've found a new place to swim, but don't tell anyone." They then gave me directions to Beaverdam Creek Reservoir, which was within a mile of their home. They said the water was much cleaner than the lake in which we normally swim, and best of all "nobody goes there!"

I meant to check it out, but put it on the back-burner until a year later when a kayaking friend and member of the Chesapeake Paddlers Association mentioned that he was meeting some other club members at Beaverdam Creek Reservoir for an evening paddle. His after-paddle report ignited my enthusiasm. It was a "must do" destination right in my own backyard – a place I could even visit easily on a weeknight!

Plans were made, and I was soon introduced to the object of all the hype. I will not go as far to say that Beaverdam was magical – but it was downright pretty and certainly a worthwhile kayaking destination.

Although it is located in Loudoun County, Beaverdam Creek Reservoir is a water supply for Fairfax County. The lake itself is 350 acres, but it is

surrounded by parkland.
There are no houses or
commercial buildings on
its shores; in fact, the only
structure around is the dam
itself.

There are three access points
to the reservoir, Mt. Hope
Road, Alford Road and
Reservoir Road. The launch
area at Mt. Hope Road is a
convenient option for kayakers since the parking area there is close to the
water. I use the term "launch area" loosely. There is no constructed ramp to
the water, but just a muddy dirt landing.

The reservoir is a popular place for local birders and the location of
documented sightings of "lifelist" birds such as several species of grebes
and the great cormorant. I have seen tundra swans there myself, which is
always a treat, but I know there are many more exciting winged residents to
discover.

The reservoir's shoreline is mostly wooded, and you will need to carry your
boat through some trees and grass to the water. The scenery is tranquil. The
water is clear enough to see through. The shoreline undulates enough for
good exploration yet the reservoir is wide enough for open water crossings.

One curious feature of Beaverdam Creek Reservoir is that the dam itself
is not marked off with buoys or anything else. You can literally paddle
right up to it. I have never noticed a current pulling me towards it, so it
is easy to paddle up to it and stop (I guess unless the wind pushes you).
Nonetheless, it is a very interesting sensation to sit near its edge (not that
I am recommending you do that – you should always stay a safe distance
away from a dam). In any case, the drop over the edge is not significant, so
it is fun to have a look.

The reservoir is officially 350 acres, and water levels can fluctuate greatly
depending on local rainfall. A thorough crawl around the shoreline can
take a couple of hours, and there are a few streams to creep up and explore.
There is visible development in the distance, but the immediate area is very
wild and peaceful.

Fishing is reported to be great in the lake, and consists of crappie, catfish,
bluegill and both largemouth and smallmouth bass.

Since there is no developed boat ramp, boating company is limited on the lake, which is another huge plus to this beautiful reservoir. If you try to search the Internet for information on the lake, be aware that there's a much better known reservoir called Beaverdam Swamp Reservoir in Gloucester County, Virginia. It is many miles away and of no relation to the little gem in Loudoun.

Directions: From the Dulles Toll Road (Route 267) in Virginia, take Exit 4 to Belmont Drive (south). Turn right on Mt. Hope Road and follow to the parking area by the water.

BURKE LAKE PARK
Body of Water: Burke Lake
County: Fairfax
Launch Type: Ramp
Launch Fee: Park Entrance is free to Fairfax County residents and $8.00
*   for non-residents. Launch fees are $5.00 (seasonal pass available)*
Restrooms: Yes
Parking: Yes

"Take the kids for the weekend? Sure, no problem," I said into the telephone as my husband looked up at me in horror from his dinner plate.

And with that, the deal was done. We were entrusted with the lives of the 10 and 11 year old children of some close friends. How hard could it be? We had known the girls their whole lives and knew they were exceptionally well behaved. Plus, we had plenty of pets, was caring for children that much different? But as the weekend drew near, I started to panic. Not only did I want to make sure the kids survived the weekend with us, I now had the desire to make it the best weekend of their lives. Something they talked about at school with their friends. I wanted to be the cool "friend of my mom's" that made them forget that their parents were having a fabulous weekend out of town without them.

My mind was blank. I couldn't think of a thing to do to entertain them. What do young girls do these days? When I was their age we went roller-skating. Do roller rinks still exist? Finally, my husband suggested we take them kayaking. I hesitated, thinking of all the possible scenarios. One capsizes and drowns while the other gets dragged off by a snapping turtle or, worse yet, a water snake. I knew they could swim, yet I worried.

The day was upon us and the girls were excited. They loved the idea of kayaking but had never tried it before. We decided to head to Burke Lake Park in Fairfax Station, Virginia. The 218-acre lake would be the perfect venue for a first kayaking experience. It was a warm spring day, and I figured there would be enough people around in case we needed an extra hand.

We looked like a kayaking outfitter as we pulled into the parking area and unloaded the four most stable kayaks we had in our garage (three ancient Wilderness Systems Seacrets, and one Wilderness Systems Pungo). In fact, several people actually asked us if we rented boats. I was tempted to say "yes" and just collect some cash and head for the carousel instead, but one look at how excited the girls were brought me back to reality.

I strapped the girls into the biggest, best, most expensive personal floatation devices I could find at the local outfitter (at least if they flipped over, we'd find them) and handed them each a paddle. After some brief stretches and some on land instruction, we headed down the boat ramp into the water.

The park was a bustle of activity as people picnicked and enjoyed a beautiful day outdoors. But once out on the water, the crowds and activity quickly evaporated into the background.

It had been some time since I had paddled in Burke Lake, and I had forgotten how beautiful it is. Although the lake is not surrounded by the ample wilderness of some other spots in the area, it is certainly pleasant and worth an afternoon of exploration. I particularly enjoy paddling there early in the season before the crowds come out, to remind my muscles of what it is like to paddle after hibernating all winter.

There were plenty of people fishing for largemouth bass, for which the lake is famous. But, since only electric motorboats are allowed on the lake, it was very quiet.

The lake is primarily tree-lined, and has many nooks and crannies to explore. The girls enjoyed looking for birds and turtles along the shore and we quietly paddled our way around the lake. Burke Lake is surrounded by a 4.68-mile loop trail, so we would occasionally see runners and walkers winding their way through the woods.

The lake is big enough for good exploration, but small enough that you will not get lost or have a difficult time getting back to the boat ramp if children get tired or the weather turns bad. However, do not be fooled by the tameness of the water. It does not take much wind to kick up some waves, and I have even been out in whitecaps before.

We spent about two hours exploring the lake, which is ample time to make your way around the 4.5 mile shoreline. I breathed a sigh of relief as we climbed out of our kayaks and freed everyone from the grip of their PFDs.

After piling all our gear into the car and strapping all the boats down, we decided to celebrate a successful outing by filling up on ice cream from the park snack bar.

Directions: From Route 495 in Virginia, take Exit 54A (Braddock Road) west. Turn left after two miles onto Burke Lake Road and then left again after five miles onto Ox Road. Follow Ox Road past the entrance to the Burke Lake golf course to the park entrance on the left.

From I-95 in Virginia, take Exit 160 (Route 123 north toward Woodbridge, Occoquan and Lakeridge). After 7.5 miles the park entrance will be on your right (7315 Ox Road). The park offers limited launching from April 1 – Memorial Day and full service from Memorial Day – Labor Day. Call 703-323-6601 for additional information.

FOUNTAINHEAD REGIONAL PARK
Body of Water: Occoquan Reservoir
County: Fairfax
Launch Type: Shoreline/Ramp
Launch Fee: $2.00 Shoreline/$5.00 Ramp
Restrooms: Yes
Parking: Yes

Fountainhead Regional Park and Bull Run Marina are two reliable destinations that consistently deliver a good paddle. They offer convenient parking, pleasant scenery and little boat traffic considering their relatively urban locations. Both are nestled on the Occoquan Reservoir in Virginia, and the paddling distance between the two is approximately five miles.

I prefer to begin my paddle from Fountainhead, which is located on Hampton Road in Fairfax Station, on the north shore of the reservoir. It is managed by the Northern Virginia Regional Park Authority. The park is probably most well known for its challenging mountain biking and running trails. The park is open mid-March through mid-November. Starting at Fountainhead, I paddle upstream to Bull Run Marina and then back again for a nice 10 mile paddle (of course, you can turn around at any point, or paddle downstream from the launch — there are several good options).

The Fountainhead boat ramp is located at the widest part of the Occoquan Reservoir. Daily and seasonal launch permits are available. Canoes are also available for rent. The reservoir forms the border between Fairfax and Prince William Counties, but the launch areas are on the Fairfax side.

The current is usually slow on the reservoir. The Occoquan River and Bull Run Creek feed into it, but even when the water is high, it is usually easy to paddle. I can't say that after a storm is the best time to go, however, since the water turns a very thick brown with a good rain. Not that it is particularly dirty; it just looks uninviting for a wet exit.

During normal water levels a ribbon of sandy shore encircles most of the reservoir. I heard from a friend who grew up in Clifton that in severe drought, the water level drops significantly, exposing wide muddy shores. I, personally, have not seen this, but my friend recalls a childhood memory of walking out onto mud flats of sorts, and becoming stuck in the mud in his yellow rubber boots. Apparently, a classic parent rescue soon followed, with him being plucked from the mud, without his boots, and carried to safety. Perhaps the boots are still there somewhere. If you find one, I will gladly give you his address.

About two miles before reaching Bull Run Marina, you will paddle by the junction of Occoquan River and Bull Run Creek. Stay right on Bull Run Creek to reach the marina. Just past the bridge on Old Yates Ford Road, you will see the floating docks at Bull Run Marina. If you are like me, you always welcome an opportunity for a clean restroom along the paddle and Bull

Run Marina seems like the natural place for a pit stop. However, as I found out the hard way one hot day while abiding by my "lots of fluids" rule, the restrooms are not always open. So plan accordingly.

On a recent paddle in high water, I went from Fountainhead to Bull Marina and back in about 3 hours. This was at a comfortable pace, with stops from time to time for snacks and bird watching. So if you are still getting a feel for how fast you paddle and how long this trip would take, this should give you some idea.

The scenery on the reservoir is suburban. There are scatterings of expensive homes that overlook the water on the western shore, but on the entire eastern shore the park borders the water. Blue heron are extremely plentiful and the overall atmosphere is relaxing. The Occoquan Reservoir is fairly wide between the two parks. It twists and turns slightly, and has one 90-degree bend. Upstream from Bull Run Marina, in Bull Run Creek, the water narrows considerably and the shoreline looks quite wild. This is another beautiful place to paddle and unwind at the end of a workday.

If you are hungry after your paddle, there's a snack bar and deck near the boat launch at Fountainhead. There are also bathroom facilities as well as bait, tackle and fishing license sales.

Directions: From I-95 in Virginia, take Exit 160 (Route 123 north toward Woodbridge, Occoquan and Lake Ridge). Turn left onto Hampton Road and continue approximately three miles to the park entrance. The park is open mid-March through mid-November from dawn to dusk. For additional information call the Northern Virginia Regional Park Authority Headquarters at 703-352-5900.

MASON NECK STATE PARK
Body of Water: Kane's Creek/Belmont Bay/Occoquan Bay/Potomac River
County: Fairfax
Launch Type: Beach
Launch Fee: $4.00 (park entrance)
Restrooms: Yes
Parking: Yes

"What is it??" I said in as loud a whisper as I could manage while paddling quickly toward my husband. He was sitting near the shore in his big yellow kayak that we affectionately call the "banana," leaning forward and peering into the grass while waving to me to come over. As I got closer, his waves stopped suddenly and he motioned for me to stay back.

"What is it?" I repeated, growing more curious as now I was told not to come over.

He looked up and smiled and said, "It's wild, but you're not going to like it." I paddled up and looked into the grass where he was pointing. A battle of nature was in full fury. A large water snake was attempting to drag a flailing fish out of the water and swallow it, and the victim was putting up a tremendous fight. He was right, of course, my squeamishness for snakes was being put to the test, yet I couldn't take my eyes off the spectacle. We watched as the snake eventually dragged the fish completely out of the water.

We went to Mason Neck to see bald eagles, but you never know what Mother Nature will serve up. I have witnessed an amazing array of wildlife there. In numerous trips over the past decade I have seen beaver, whistling swans, osprey and numerous bald eagles, to name a few.

Mason Neck is located on a peninsula that is bordered by the Potomac River to the east, Pohick Bay to the north and Belmont Bay to the south. It is connected to a National Wildlife Refuge for a combined total of more than 2,000 acres. The park contains hundreds of acres of hardwood forests and is home to an active heron rookery.

Plans for the park began in the mid 1960's, when two bald eagle nests were discovered on the peninsula. The nests were a significant discovery since bald eagles were extremely rare in this region at the time. Logging in the area during the late 1800's and early 1900's and the use of pesticides destroyed much of the natural habitat of the eagle in Virginia. Although land was purchased for the park beginning in 1967, a number of development challenges threatened the park in the following years. Mason Neck State Park finally opened to the public in 1985. It is named after George Mason IV who wrote the Virginia Declaration of Rights and lived at nearby Gunston Hall Plantation (which is now open to the public).

With respect to launch sites, there is a sandy car-top launch area on a beach at Belmont Bay that I recommend for kayaks. From there you can paddle into the marsh of Kane's Creek (to the right), or out into Belmont Bay, or left into Occoquan Bay (toward the Potomac River). In Belmont and Occoquan Bays there are numerous high bluffs and clay cliffs to scan for signs of birds and other wildlife, or to look at the interesting trees that have fallen along the bluffs.

Kane's Creek is a tidal stream and at low tide your trip up the creek can end abruptly since the water levels get very low. In the summer Kane's Creek is thick with aquatic plants and can be hard to paddle, but it is worth the extra effort. Osprey nests are scattered around the mouth of the creek. Be sure to keep a good distance away, Osprey will not hesitate to guard their nests if they feel threatened.

Bald eagles are usually easy to spot around Mason Neck. In fact, a little less than a mile up Kane's Creek is a protected nesting area for eagles. Posted signs will inform you to turn your boat around as you approach, but listen for their delicate calls (deceivingly delicate for a bird that can grow to a wingspan of eight feet!). The juveniles have dark heads, so be on the lookout for them as well as for their "bald" parents.

If you head into the Occoquan Bay and the Potomac, you will have the opportunity to practice open water paddling. On windy days, the water can be wavy and on several occasions, I have encountered large whitecaps.

For an enjoyable half day paddle, begin at Mason Neck and paddle through Occoquan Bay and into the Occoquan River. The river takes you under

Route I-95 and to the town of Occoquan, which has undergone extensive rebuilding on the waterfront over the past several years. Be aware of boat traffic coming in and out of the many marinas along the way. Also, bring a lot of water and food on hot days, since tides and wind can change directions and you can find your return trip taking a lot longer than you expected.

Directions: Mason Neck is located in southern Fairfax County, approximately 20 miles south of Washington, D.C. From Route 1 south, turn left onto Route 242 (Gunston Road) and continue five miles to the park entrance. Head toward the Visitors Center and follow the signs to the car-top launch area. For additional information call 703-339-2385.

ADDITIONAL LAUNCH SITES

NAME: POINT OF ROCKS
Body of Water: Potomac River
County: Loudoun
Launch Type: Ramp
Launch Fee: None
Restrooms: None
Parking: Yes

Directions: From Route 15 north in Virginia, Follow Route 15 north from Leesburg to the Point of Rocks Bridge. The launch is before the bridge on the last turn-off on the left (Lovettsville Road). Turn left on Lovettsville Road and then take an immediate right by the Public Boat Landing sign. Follow the road to the boat ramp.

Description: This boat ramp provides nice access to the Point of Rocks area of the Potomac River on the Virginia side of the Route 15 bridge. When the water levels are suitable for paddling, you can paddle downstream past Algonkian Park in Loudoun County. See a detailed description of paddling from Point of Rocks in the chapter on Howard, Montgomery and Frederick Counties.

NAME: *RIVER BEND PARK*
Body of Water: Potomac River
County: Fairfax
Launch Type: Ramp
Launch Fee: $5.00 (season passes available)
Restrooms: Yes
Parking: Yes

Directions: From The Capital Belway (Route 495) in Virginia, take Exit 44 west to Route 193 (Georgetown Pike). Continue past the entrance to Great Falls Park to River Bend Road. Turn right on River Bend Road and continue 2.2 miles to Jeffery Road. Turn right on Jeffery Road and continue 1 mile to the park entrance.

Description: River Bend Park is a hidden gem in Great Falls. The park contains a convenient ramp for launching, although the many rocks in the section of the Potomac that runs by the park can make for tedious paddling in low water. Paddle upstream and explore nearby islands. One mile down river from the park is a dam. The dam is marked by buoys, but do not venture near it, the current can be strong. Kayaks are available for rent at the Visitors Center. The boat ramp is closed when water levels are high. Call 703-759-9018 for details.

NAME: *LAKE FAIRFAX REGIONAL PARK*
Body of Water: Lake Fairfax
County: Fairfax
Launch Type: Floating Dock/Beach
Launch Fee: $2.00
Restrooms: Yes
Parking: Yes

Directions: From Route 495 in Virginia, take Exit 47A to Route 7 west. Continue to the intersection of Route 7 and Route 606. Turn left on Baron Cameron Avenue and then turn left onto Lake Fairfax Drive (1400 Lake Fairfax Drive).

Description: Lake Fairfax is a small 18-acre lake located in Reston, Virginia in Lake Fairfax Park. The small lake is a great place for children and beginning paddlers to practice their skills. There's also a small water park, carousel and camping on the 476-acre property. Call 703-471-5415 for additional information.

NAME: LAKE ACCOTINK PARK
Body of Water: Lake Accotink
County: Fairfax
Launch Type: Beach
Launch Fee: None
Restrooms: Yes
Parking: Yes

Directions: From I-95 in Virginia, take the exit for Old Keene Mill Road (west). Turn right on Hanover Avenue and then left onto Highland Avenue. Turn right on Accotink Park Road. Follow to the park entrance.

Description: Lake Accotink is a small 55-acre lake located in Springfield, Virginia. The lake is a great place for children and beginning kayakers to practice their skills. Kayak instruction is offered at the park through the L.L. Bean store in Tysons Corner. For additional information on park hours, call 703-569-3464.

NAME: POHICK BAY REGIONAL PARK
Body of Water: Pohick Bay/Potomac River
County: Fairfax
Launch Type: Ramp / Beach
Launch Fee: $8.00 (ramp) / $3.50 (car-top area)
Restrooms: Yes
Parking: Yes

Directions: From I-95 in Virginia, take the exit for Lorton and turn left on Lorton Road. At the third traffic light, turn right onto Lorton Market Street. Follow Lorton Market Street to the first traffic light (Route 1) and cross Route 1 to continue on Gunston Road. Follow to the park entrance (6501 Pohick Bay Drive).

Description: Launching from Pohick Bay Regional Park in Lorton, Virginia offers a scenic opportunity for a 10-mile paddle past Hallowing Point, the

Great Marsh, Fort Belvoir and Gunston Hall (home of George Mason). Kayak rentals are available in the park, as well as guided trips.

NAME: BULL RUN MARINA
Body of Water: Occoquan Reservoir and Bull Run Creek
County: Fairfax
Launch Type: Ramp/Floating Docks
Launch Fee: Seasonal pass of $35.00 (county residents)
  $47.00 (non-county residents), plus $10.00 Gate Key
Restrooms: Yes
Parking: Yes

Directions: From I-66 west in Virginia, exit on Route 123 south and continue to Clifton Road. Turn right on Clifton Road, then left on Henderson Road. Turn right on Old Yates Ford Road. Continue to Bull Run Marina.

From I-95 in Virginia, take Exit 160 (Route 123 north toward Woodbridge, Occoquan and Lakeridge). Turn left onto Henderson Road, then left onto Old Yates Ford Road and continue to the park entrance.

Description: Bull Run Marina offers another excellent launch point to Occoquan Reservoir and Bull Run Creek. However, to launch from Bull Run Marina, you must first purchase a $35.00 seasonal launch permit from Fountainhead Park (the pass is good for Bull Run Marina, Fountainhead Park and Algonkian Park). You will also need to purchase a gate key to the ramp at Bull Run Marina for an additional $10.00.

Paddle to the right to explore Bull Run Creek (which runs into the Occoquan Reservoir) and paddle left to head toward Fountainhead Regional Park. Bull Run Creek narrows significantly, but is very inviting for shoreline exploration. The marina is open mid-March through mid-November from dawn to dusk. For additional information call the Northern Virginia Regional Park Authority Headquarters at 703-352-5900.

NAME: OCCOQUAN REGIONAL PARK
Body of Water: Occoquan River
County: Fairfax
Launch Type: Ramp
Launch Fee: $3.50
Restrooms: Yes
Parking: Yes

Directions: From I-95 in Virginia, take Exit 160 north (Route 123). Cross over the Occoquan River and turn right at the traffic light onto Occoquan Regional Park Road.

Description: Occoquan Regional Park provides excellent access to the Occoquan River. You can paddle downstream through Belmont Bay to Mason Neck and the Potomac River or upstream slightly past the historic section of Occoquan. Be careful of boat traffic in the area during the season. The park offers many amenities including a snack bar, picnic pavilion, batting cages, etc.

NAME: BELLE HAVEN MARINA
Body of Water: Potomac River/Cameron Run
County: Fairfax
Launch Type: Ramp
Launch Fee: $5.00
Restrooms: Yes
Parking: Yes

Directions: Belle Haven Marina is located on Belle Haven Road, just south of Old Town Alexandria off the George Washington Parkway. Traveling south on the George Washington Parkway, pass Reagan National Airport. Stay on the parkway (it will become Washington Street in Alexandria). Turn left into Belle Haven Marina.

Description: Belle Haven Marina is a full service boating facility that rents kayaks and is home to the largest sailing school in the D.C. area. It is located on property belonging to the National Park Service. Paddle out on the Potomac and explore the Alexandria shoreline or head into Cameron Run. You can also paddle up the Potomac River all the way to Georgetown (9.5 miles).

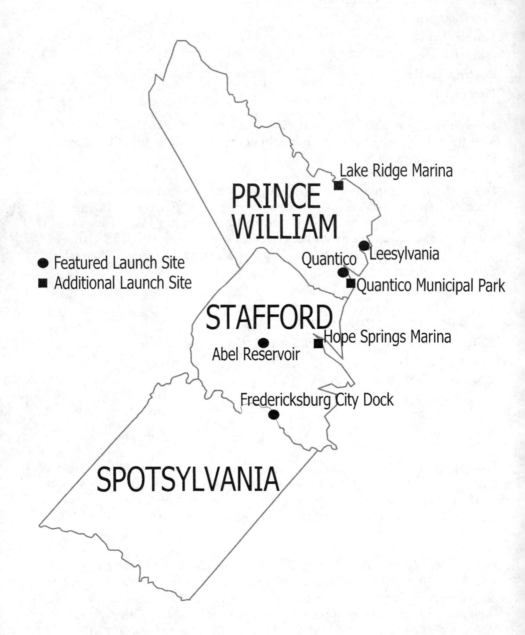

PRINCE
WILLIAM

Lake Ridge Marina

● Featured Launch Site
■ Additional Launch Site

Leesylvania
Quantico
Quantico Municipal Park

STAFFORD

Hope Springs Marina
Abel Reservoir

Fredericksburg City Dock

SPOTSYLVANIA

CHAPTER 7

PRINCE WILLIAM, STAFFORD AND SPOTSYLVANIA COUNTIES

QUANTICO MARINE BASE
Body of Water: Potomac River / Quantico Creek
County: Prince William
Launch Type: Ramp
Launch Fee: None
Restrooms: None
Parking: Yes

"It reminds me of an old Western town" is how my friend Clark describes the town of Quantico. "Like a set in *Blazing Saddles*."

I thought that sounded like a strange way to describe an East Coast military town, but arriving at the gates to the Quantico Marine Corps Base for the first time (civilians must provide identification before driving through the entrance) I kept my eyes pealed for Mel Brooks.

Eyeing the kayaks on top of our car, the friendly Marine at the gate gave my husband directions to the local marina. The first few miles on the road into Quantico are through a wooded area, but we soon turned onto Potomac Avenue and headed toward the Potomac River. Arriving "downtown," Clark's analogy was clear. The main strip in Quantico looked old and dusty, and all of the buildings were painted a drab brown. But instead of gun slinging cowboys roaming the streets, there were dozens of Marines—most of them fit, young and rather good looking.

We continued on toward the marina, but were unsure where to launch, since the facility looked like it catered mostly to private military boat owners. As we sat in the car looking at our map, a man pulled up next to us, got out of his car and approached us. "Are you looking for a place to dump those things?" he asked, pointing to our boats. We told him that we were. He then reached into his pocket and produced a badge, identifying himself as a police sergeant with the local force. He then told us where the local boat launches were and how to get there. While he was giving us directions, a police cruiser pulled up alongside our car and the two officers exchanged greetings and a few words about us needing a place to launch.

"Do you want me to take you there?" asked the second officer with regards to one of the launch sites. Before we could answer, he continued, "Here, follow me – I'll show you." With that he motioned for us to turn our car around and follow his lead. As we started the car, the sergeant told us to stop by the police station after our paddle for a cup of coffee, and handed us his business card. What followed was our first (and only, to date) police escort to a boat ramp.

Quantico is bordered to the east by the Potomac River, and the boat launch recommended to us by the local authorities is one we've used several times since as a good launch point to explore the area. The ramp is located on the Marine Corps Systems Command grounds at the mouth of Quantico Creek where it meets the Potomac.

The launch is a no-frills facility. You will find parking and a cement ramp, but no restrooms or other amenities. It is free to launch and the local flavor is free as well. Each time I have gone to Quantico, I've seen or met interesting characters at the launch. My favorites were a couple of young 20-something men who were skipping work to sit in their Cadillac Seville listening to high volume heavy metal music while singing and banging their heads. Wayne and Garth could not have done it any better. While I was considering heading for another launch site, the driver door opened and smoke poured out of the car. Then the driver approached me, still singing along with his music and asked if I needed help unloading my boat from on top of my car. After a few polite exchanges, he returned to his head-banging passenger and I heard him say, "Dude, when we get money we're going to get those canoe-rafting things and a cool truck just like that!"

One thing is for sure, whether it be the local law enforcement or the potential enforcee, I have not met anyone in Quantico who wasn't friendly and helpful.

The cement ramp often has natural debris on it, so watch for rocks and sticks when you launch. There is a train bridge next to the launch area where Amtrak and commuter trains run at regular intervals. There are two choices for paddling from the launch — to the left up Quantico Creek or to the right, into the Potomac River. Both offer interesting shoreline. I usually choose my route after seeing which way the wind and current are flowing. The Quantico Creek can sometimes be rougher than the much larger Potomac, depending on wind speed and direction. Exploring the creek is a fine way to view wildlife, but I actually prefer to head around the point of land marking the mouth of the creek and into the Potomac.

Give the shoreline a bit of a berth as you round the bend into the Potomac. The closer you hug the shore the greater chance you have of coming in contact with rocks. Soon after entering the Potomac, you can paddle downstream into a protected cove by the Municipal Park. There is another launch site in the park which is protected on one side by the point of land leading into Quantico Creek, and on the other by the local marina.

The marina at Quantico is protected by a cement seawall. There are often sea birds such as cormorants hanging out at the entrance to the marina. If passing boaters have any doubt about their location, a quick glance at the marina wall will erase any uncertainty. "QUANTICO" is painted in large white letters on the wall facing out into the river.

The Potomac is very wide around Quantico, so rather than paddling across, I normally paddle out to Chopawamsic Island, which is a 13-acre private island located less than 300 yards from shore. There are several houses on the island that can be seen from the water, but there is no place for the public to land. It is approximately 1 ¾ miles from the launch to the island.

The shoreline is a mix of trees and drab military buildings, but the undulating shoreline makes for a great place to practice open water paddling. I have sea kayaked in Quantico in all seasons, and it is always an enjoyable experience. The company on the water is a nice mix of paddlers and pleasure boaters, and I have found everyone to be courteous and friendly.

Directions: From Route I-95 in Virginia, take Exit 150A (Route 619 east). Route 619 becomes Fuller Road (access through the Marine Corps Base entrance – have your driver's license ready to display to the guards). Bear right onto Barnett Avenue and turn left on Potomac Avenue at the traffic light. Turn left on River Road and continue past the park through the gate to the Marine Corps Systems Command. The road turns into Sherwood Avenue. Turn left on Halyburton Street. Follow around the corner to the right then follow the sign to the boat ramp.

LEESYLVANIA STATE PARK
Body of Water: Potomac River
County: Prince William
Launch Facilities: Beach
Launch Fee: $3.00
Restrooms: Yes
Parking: Yes

The history of Leesylvania State Park dates back to colonial times when Revolutionary War hero Henry Lee III (known as Light Horse Harry) was born in the Leesylvania Plantation house. He would later father Civil War General Robert E. Lee. Ruins of the plantation house and several graves still remain on the property.

Leesylvania is a relatively new park, opening in 1992 a little more than a decade after the land was donated to the Commonwealth of Virginia. The park consists of 508 acres in southeast Prince William County and sits on a peninsula bordered by three bodies of water, the Potomac River, Neabsco Creek, and Powells Creek.

When you arrive at the park entrance, a ranger will collect the $3.00 parking fee. Follow the road into the park. Before you reach the boat ramp, you will see the gravel road leading to the car-top launch area on Powell's Creek. There is a small parking area near the car-top launch. Unload your boat and then move your car to the lot. In the past, there has been a portable toilet by the car-top parking, but permanent facilities are located by the park store, which is open from April through October. There is also a snack bar at the store and they sell bait and limited groceries.

Leesylvania offers some varied paddling options. Depending on your mood (or how experienced you are), you can explore the calm, sheltered marsh in Powell's Creek, or navigate open water currents and boat traffic in the Potomac.

A paddle up Powell's Creek (to the right of the boat launch and under the railroad bridge), brings you to the start of a large marsh area. Tall pilings are located in the creek to attract ospreys and encourage them to breed. It is an ideal location for viewing these birds and their nests, but do not get too near, especially when their chicks are newly hatched. I learned this the hard way, while trying to photograph them on one of my first trips to the area.

Osprey give plenty of warning when they feel threatened, so if you approach a nest and mom or dad bird start fussing at you (often they will fly around the nest as you approach, calling), back off. They will not hesitate to dive at you if you end up right under their nesting area. During my own encounter, I not only felt terrible about disturbing them, but I also feared for a moment that they might actually hurt me. In any case, the point was well taken, and I purchased a better camera with a powerful telephoto lens and now keep my distance.

Paddle into the marsh and look for signs of beaver, nutria and water fowl. The slower you move the better chance you have for catching a glimpse of something cute and wild. Turtles are common residents in the marsh although they can be hard to see through the similarly shaped lily pads.

Depending on your available time, you can either head toward the open waters of the Potomac by passing around Bushey Point (east of the car-top launch), or save that for another day. Once you round the point, be prepared for windy conditions and boat traffic. Unless you have a particularly calm day on the water, you can also expect to face noticeable currents.

The Potomac is tidal in this area, but is considered to be fresh water. The area is excellent for largemouth bass fishing but catfish, perch and striped bass also populate the water. Be sure to pick up a Virginia freshwater fishing license if you plan to bring your rod and reel.

Following the shoreline past Bushey Point, you will paddle by the main boat launch and large rocks that act as breakers protecting the marina. On a nice summer day, be especially careful of boats entering and exiting the marina, unfortunately not all are courteous of kayaks and there are no horsepower restrictions on motors.

Pass the marina and continue along the shoreline. Again, depending on your time and energy constraints, you can continue on to "Freestone Point," which is recognizable by its rock cliffs. Freestone Point garnered its name after the sandstone found and removed there by early settlers for use as building material.

Before reaching the point, there is a half mile of sandy beach along the park shore. Swimming is prohibited, though it is tempting on a hot summer day.

If you are feeling adventurous and wish to continue past the point, you can do a fun open water crossing over to Featherstone Wildlife Refuge. During the crossing, if the visibility is good, you can see the cliffs at Mason Neck to the north.

Directions: Leesylvania State Park is located about halfway between Washington, D.C. and Fredericksburg, off Route I-95. From I-95, take Exit 156 (Rippon Landing) east to Route 784. Take 784 to U.S. 1 (turn right on Route 1) to Route 610 (Neabsco Road). Follow to the park entrance. For additional information call 703-670-0372.

ABEL RESERVOIR
Body of Water: Abel Reservoir
County: Stafford
Launch Facilities: Ramp
Launch Fee: None
Restrooms: None
Parking: Yes

I have to admit, Abel Reservoir holds a special place in my heart. It is where I truly discovered my love for sea kayaking. Many years ago, after trying our hand at the sport one time in the Outer Banks of North Carolina, my husband and I purchased a couple of Wilderness Systems Seacrets and brought them to our then home in Stafford County, Virginia. Our own sea kayaks – how exciting! We could kayak anytime we wanted to! The next question was – where? We did not live near the beach – and we really didn't know of any local lakes since we had recently moved to the county. Long summer days would allow us a little time to paddle in the evenings – but not much since our long commute from D.C. ate up much of the daylight. Then we discovered Abel Reservoir.

When we scanned the local map, I was less than enthusiastic. We saw Abel Reservoir (which is a water supply for Stafford County) not far from our home and considered if it was an option. How nice could a reservoir be? How big was it? It looked fairly sizable on the map, so we loaded up our boats and decided to check it out. Our first ray of hope came in the form of a well-kept boat ramp with free parking and launching. Nice! A little sign was posted detailing what types of boats were allowed on the water (no power motors), and it also explained that the launch site could only be used during the daylight. Great – we fit the requirements!

We eagerly unloaded our boats, and parked the car next to a handful of pick-up trucks and small boat trailers.

The launch area was neat and clean and except for the occasional car passing over a bridge near the launch site, it was very, very quiet. We carefully launched our new boats (not wanting to scratch our new favorite toys) and slipped into the still water. The launch site is located at the northern end of the lake, so there was only one obvious direction to paddle.

The shore was lined with trees, noticeably hemlock. It actually looked a lot like what I picture when I think of North Country and Canadian lakes, although the humidity of the summer day somewhat diminished the vision. The banks in most places were fairly steep with rocky outcrops, but with room to land if we experienced a crisis. There were a few houses scattered in the trees, but most were barely visible and were situated high on the banks.

The lake's 185 acres were stretched out over three miles (6 miles round trip), but you could add an extra mile to that if you explore all the offshoots and bays. Although somewhat narrow in a few places and generally long and curvy, the shoreline made the paddle interesting since the view changed frequently. The water did open up quite a bit in several areas, providing nice wide views of the mostly undeveloped shoreline.

The only other people on the lake were in a handful of small fishing boats, but there was plenty of company. Blue herons, Canada geese, cormorants, red tail hawks and a variety of other birds accompanied us on our paddle and spotting wildlife was easy. We even saw a large beaver who turned away from us, slapped the water with his tail, and dove underwater.

I am not a fisherman, or fisherwoman I guess I should say, but based on the success of the people we saw fishing in the lake, I would recommend it if that is your sport. The Virginia Department of Game & Inland Fisheries says there are largemouth bass in the reservoir as well as good crappie and chain pickerel populations (with pickerel up to three pounds caught there annually). They also note a significant bluegills and channel catfish population.

After our maiden voyage on Abel Reservoir, we routinely returned during the two years we lived in Stafford. Back then, sea kayaking was still very new to the area and I can not recall ever seeing another kayak there. People would always look at our boats with funny expressions and would often ask questions about them.

Having long since moved from Stafford back up to Northern Virginia in Reston, it had been at least 10 years since our last paddle on Abel Reservoir. I had such fond memories of the place though that I could not wait to return to see if it was really as wonderful as I remembered, or if I just did not have much to compare it to at the time.

Driving down Route I-95 with my husband and another paddling friend, I was struck with an unsettling thought. What if the lakeshore was now full of houses? At the rate of development in Stafford County, I was sure that my 10-year absence would have been ample time for a dramatic change in scenery. Biting my nails as we drove past a patchwork vista of rooftops that we remembered as treetops near our old neighborhood, the reality of this possibility became quite clear. As we turned down Route 651, however, my anxiety subsided some as the old familiar farmhouses came into sight and the area regained its rural ambiance. We all heaved a sigh of relief when we turned into the old familiar parking area – which looked the same as the day we moved. There was one notable difference, however, the driver of a car idling at the gravel launch ramp smiled and waved as we pulled in – and then turned to un-strap the two kayaks on top of his car.

One thing worth mentioning is that aquatic plants have recently moved into the shallows of the lake. So it is best to go early in the season before it takes hold. Paddling is still good there later in the summer, but you will have to slog your paddle through the aquatic plants near the launch area until you enter deeper water.

Directions: From Route I-95 in Virginia, take Exit 140 west in Stafford (Route 630) to Courthouse Road. Turn left onto Ramoth Church Road (Route 628). Turn right onto Kellogg Mill Road (Route 651). After crossing over Abel Reservoir, turn right at the entrance to the boat ramp.

FREDERICKSBURG CITY DOCK
Body of Water: Rappahannock River
County: Spotsylvania
Launch Type: Ramp
Launch Fee: None
Restrooms: Yes (portable)
Parking: Yes

Fredericksburg bills itself as the "Most Historical City in America." This doesn't seem like much of a stretch given that it has ties to both the Revolutionary and Civil Wars.

Because of its central location to both Washington, D.C. and Richmond, Virginia and its location on the Rappahannock River, Fredericksburg became a natural shipping hub in the mid-1700's. Over the years, many famous historical figures allegedly lived in Fredericksburg, including George Washington, John Paul Jones and James Monroe.

The most well-known historical features in the area are the numerous battlefields in and around the city. Several very important battles were fought in Fredericksburg during the Civil War, including a battle between Confederate and Union troops for rival capitals.

Fredericksburg is easily accessed from Route I-95. The quaint historic district is a popular tourist destination for Washingtonians, and it is also a popular stopping point for people traveling on I-95. The students from nearby University of Mary Washington provide the workforce for many part-time jobs in charming stores and eateries along central Princess Anne Street and adjacent roads. You can find everything there from exclusive "made in Virginia" arts and crafts to delicious ice cream in quaint parlors reminiscent of the 40s and 50s.

The town sits along the banks of the Rappahannock River and includes blocks of historic residences from the 18th and 19th centuries. A few of the homes even have real cannonballs still stuck in the sides of them – authentic reminders of days when things were not so pleasant around the beautiful town.

The City Dock offers the best access to the Rappahannock River. Follow the banks of the river east along Sophia Street. The road dead-ends at the Fredericksburg City Dock. It will be easy to identify, since an old-fashioned touring paddlewheel boat is often docked there. There are two boat ramps. Choose one and unload your gear, then leave your car in the well-maintained parking area. There are no fulltime restroom facilities, but there is normally a portable toilet available.

I lived in the Fredericksburg area for a few years, and was amazed by the many moods of the Rappahannock River. The low banks along the northern shore near town surrender frequently to flood waters and, at times, the City Dock itself has been under water. Flooding is most frequent in the springtime. At most other times of the year, the river provides a quiet venue for a leisurely paddle.

The first time I launched from the City Dock, I was surprised at the number of powerboats in the launch area. I soon learned that the City Dock is a jump-off point to the Chesapeake Bay. It would be a multi-day trip in a kayak, but is certainly not out of the question if you are feeling adventurous and have the time.

Last time I launched at the City Dock, a pair of extremely friendly white ducks greeted me at the ramp, clearly convinced that I would deliver their lunch. They were picture perfect, like they just walked out of a children's book. After waddling right up to my feet and staring hopefully at me for quite some time, they finally resigned themselves that there would not be a free snack and returned to the water.

The two obvious choices for paddling are upstream and downstream. Each have their plusses. If you head upstream (to the left), you can paddle past Old Town, but be prepared to see a different side of Fredericksburg. Although the town is on the river, it sadly doesn't have the waterfront appeal you might expect. There are several gorgeous historical homes along the shore and a number of restored buildings and restaurants, including some truly uniquely renovated industrial buildings that are now private homes. Much of the waterfront, however, is wildly overgrown and there are many abandoned businesses from a day long ago, including the old town power company building which rests along the shore with broken windows and empty floors.

Even so, the paddle upstream is very pleasant. In low water, several islands poke out of the river and motorboats are not able to navigate the shallow water. So even in summer, you can be alone on the river, except for a passing duck or heron.

Paddling upstream from the City Dock, you will soon pass under a well traveled railroad bridge. The design of this bridge is one of my favorites. The wide arches underneath the bridge are impressive from below and the bridge supports have high ledges that often have giant trees balanced across them – a stark reminder of the power of flood waters.

Upstream from the railroad bridge is another less impressive highway overpass that leads into the old town from the direction of Falmouth, Virginia. The north shore of the river will seem wild and empty in the summer. The underbrush shields a road that runs along the river. There is a park and some houses owned by hardy souls along the road. I say they are hardy because I've witnessed first hand the battle they sometimes lose against nature when floodwaters force them from their homes.

Depending on water levels, the paddle upstream is usually no more than a mile or two since shallow water usually forces an early return trip somewhere around the Route 1 bridge.

Paddling downstream from the City Dock is a good option if you have a longer paddle in mind. You will be joined by more boat traffic on nice days, but the river is usually wide and lazy with room for everyone.

The trip downstream is optimal for viewing birds and other wildlife, such as deer and turtles. There are also several plantation-style homes you can see clearly from the water and ruins of buildings from earlier days.

The Rappahannock River, although once a major shipping highway and certainly an important artery in the Virginia countryside, gets little recognition these days compared to its sister river the Potomac. Its banks have remained relatively undeveloped compared to most waterways in the mid-Atlantic, which allows for miles of uninterrupted paddling in a very pleasant environment.

Do not let your trip to Fredericksburg end when your paddle trip is through. Head into old town for a great meal at Sammy T's and then on to perhaps the most notorious ice cream stand in Virginia--Carl's on Princess Anne Street. Carl's is truly a favorite landmark for residents and visitors. Do not be scared off if the line of eager patrons (which will no doubt include everyone from your grandmother to tattoo clad bikers, police officers and small children) wraps around the building. The folks who scoop ice cream at Carl's are professionals and the line will move quickly (just have your money and order ready when you approach the window).

Directions: From Route I-95 in Virginia, take Exit 133A for Route 17 (toward Falmouth). Turn right on Route 1 and cross the bridge over the Rappahannock River. Turn left at the next traffic light onto Princess Anne Street. Once in Old Town, turn left on Hanover Street and then right on Sophia Street. Follow Sophia Street to the City Dock.

ADDITIONAL LAUNCH SITES

NAME: LAKE RIDGE MARINA
Body of Water: Occoquan Reservoir
County: Prince William
Launch Type: Ramp
Launch Fee: $5.00
Restrooms: Yes
Parking: Yes

Directions: From Route I-95 in Virginia, take Exit 160 north (Route 123). Turn left at the second traffic light onto Old Bridge Road. Go approximately five miles and turn right onto Hedges Run Road. Turn left onto Cotton Mill Road. Follow to the Lake Ridge Park entrance (12350 Cotton Mill Drive).

Description: Launch on the Occoquan Reservoir. The park is a full service facility with fishing, boating, hiking trails, picnic pavilions, playground, golf course, etc. The marina is open on weekends starting in April, daily from mid-June through September and weekends until the beginning of October. Call 703-494-5288 for additional information.

NAME: TOWN OF QUANTICO MUNICIPAL PARK
Body of Water: Potomac River
County: Prince William
Launch Type: Beach
Launch Fee: None
Restrooms: None
Parking: Yes

Directions: From Route I-95 in Virginia, take Exit 150A (Route 619) east. Route 619 becomes Fuller Road (access through the Marine Corps Base entrance – have your driver's license ready to display to the guards). Bear right onto Barnett Avenue and turn left on Potomac Avenue at the traffic light. Turn left on River Road and follow to the park on left.

Description: This is a second good launch point available to the public on the marine base. Park behind the tennis courts and launch on the sandy beach into a somewhat protected bay next to the local marina. Access is directly on the Potomac River. The river is wide at this point. Paddle on the Potomac, or upstream to the left to access Occoquan Creek.

NAME: HOPE SPRINGS MARINA
Body of Water: Aquia Creek
County: Stafford
Launch Type: Ramp
Launch Fee: $5.00 (car-top)
Restrooms: Yes
Parking: Yes

Directions: From Route I-95 in Virginia, take Exit 140 east in Stafford. Turn left on Route 1 (the courthouse will be on your left). Turn right at the next light onto Hope Road. Follow Hope Road 3 ½ miles to the Hope Springs Marina sign. Continue to the marina on Hope Springs Lane (4 Hope Springs Lane).

Description: Hope Springs Marina is a full service marina providing access primarily to power boats. Launch at the ramp into Aquia Creek. Explore

Aquia Creek in both directions, or paddle downstream into the Potomac River. Call 540-659-1128 for additional information on the marina.

PADDLING RESOURCES

BALTIMORE/WASHINGTON, D.C. AREA OUTFITTERS

Please note that some of the following businesses are seasonal. Please call ahead for information on specific hours of operation and details on services.

DISTRICT OF COLUMBIA AND ARLINGTON

Eastern Mountain Sports (EMS)
The Market Common
2800 Clarendon Boulevard, Suite R550
Arlington, VA 22201
703-248-8310
www.ems.com
Kayak Sales, Rentals

Hudson Trail Outfitters, LTD. (HTO)
Pentagon Row
1101 South Joyce Street, Suite B29
Arlington VA 22202
703-415-4861
www.hudsontrail.com
Kayak Sales

Hudson Trail Outfitters, LTD. (HTO)
Tenley Circle
4530 Wisconsin Avenue, N.W.
Washington, DC 20016
202-363-9810
www.hudsontrail.com
Kayak Sales

Jack's Boathouse
3500 K Street, NW
Washington, D.C. 20007
202-337-9624
www.jacksboathouse.com
Kayak Rentals, Instruction

Outdoor Excursions
1-800-77-KAYAK
www.outdoorexcursions.com
Kayak Instruction, Guided Tours

Potomac Paddlesports
301-881-2628
www.potomacpaddlesports.com
Kayak Instruction, Guided Tours

REI
800-622-2236
www.rei.com/adventures
Kayak Tours

The Pathfinder Group
1114 East Capital Street NE
Washington, DC 20002
202-546-0269
www.washpathfind.com
Kayak Instruction, Guided Tours, Environmental Interpretation

Thompson Boat Center
2900 Virginia Ave., NW
Washington, DC 20037
202-333-9543
www.thompsonboatcenter.com
Kayak Rentals

BALTIMORE, HARFORD AND CARROLL COUNTIES

Autumn Sky Outfitters
3404 Conowingo Road
Street, MD 21154
410-836-3660
www.autumnskyoutfitters.com
Kayak Sales, Rentals

Baltimore Sailing Center
Rocky Point Park
2200 Rocky Point Road
Essex, MD 21221
410-391-0196
www.bcsailing.org
Kayak Instruction

Hudson Trail Outfitters, LTD. (HTO)
424 York Road
Towson, MD 21204
410-583-0494
www.hudsontrail.com
Kayak Sales

REI
63 W Aylesbury Rd
Timonium, MD 21093
410-252-5920
www.rei.com
Kayak Sales

Ultimate Watersports
Gunpowder Falls State Park
Hammerman Area
7200 Graces Quarters Road
Baltimore, MD 21220
410-335-5352
www.ultimatewatersports.com
Kayak Rentals, Instruction, Guided Tours, Summer Camps

Ultimate Watersports
Gunpowder Falls State Park
Dundee Creek Marina
7400 Graces Quarters Road
Baltimore, MD 21220
410-335-5352
www.ultimatewatersports.com
Kayak Rentals, Instruction, Guided Tours, Summer Camps

Starrk Moon Kayaks Inc. (York County)
497 Cold Cabin Road
Delta, PA 17314
717-456-7720
www.starrkmoon.com
Kayak Sales, Rentals

HOWARD, MONTGOMERY AND FREDERICK COUNTIES

Hudson Trail Outfitters, LTD. (HTO)
401 N. Frederick Avenue
Gaithersburg MD 20879
301-948-2474
www.hudsontrail.com
Kayak Sales

Hudson Trail Outfitters, LTD. (HTO)
12085 Rockville Pike
Rockville MD 20852
301-881-4955
www.hudsontrail.com
Kayak Sales

L.L. Bean
10300 Little Patuxent Parkway
Columbia, MD 21044
410-715-7020
www.llbean.com
Kayak Sales, Instruction

Potomac Paddlesports
11917 Maple Ave
Rockville, MD 20852
301-881-2628
www.potomacpaddlesports.com
Kayak Sales

REI
1701 Rockville Pike
Rockville, MD 20852
301-230-7670
www.rei.com
Kayak Sales

River & Trail Outfitters (Washington County)
604 Valley Road
Knoxville, MD 21758
888-446-7529
301-695-5177
www.rivertrail.com
Kayak Sales, Rentals, Guided Tours

ANNE ARUNDEL, CHARLES AND PRINCE GEORGE'S COUNTIES

Annapolis Canoe and Kayak
311 Third Street
Annapolis, MD 21403
410-263-2303
www.annapoliscanoeandkayak.com
Kayak Sales, Rentals

Atlantic Kayak Company
Fort Washington Marina
13600 King Charles Terrace
Fort Washington, MD 20744
301-292-6455
www.atlantickayak.com
Kayak Sales, Rentals, Instruction, Guided Tours

Beacon Surplus
3256 Leonardtown Rd
Waldorf, MD 20601
301-645-0077
www.beaconsurplus.com
Kayak Sales

Chesapeake Light Craft LLC
1805 George Avenue
Annapolis, MD 21401
410-267-0137
www.CLCboats.com
Kayak Builder, Kayak Kit Sales

Chesapeake Paddlesports
410-224-7822
www.chesapeakepaddlesports.com
Kayak Sales, Instruction, Guided Tours

Eastern Mountain Sports (EMS)
Annapolis Harbour Center
2554 Solomons Island Road
Annapolis, MD 21401
410-573-1240
www.ems.com
Kayak Sales, Rentals

Hudson Trail Outfitters, LTD. (HTO)
Annapolis Mall
1079 Annapolis Mall
Annapolis MD 21401
410-266-8390
www.hudsontrail.com
Kayak Sales

KayakTraining.com
410-790-0203
www.kayaktraining.com
Kayak Instruction, Guided Tours

L.L. Bean Paddling Center
Chesapeake Bay Foundation's
Philip Merrill Environmental Center
888-552-3261
www.llbean.com/ods
Kayak Instruction, Guided Tours

REI
9801 Rhode Island Ave
(Hollywood Plaza)
College Park, MD 20740
301-982-9681
www.rei.com
Kayak Sales

REI
800-622-2236
www.rei.com/adventures
Kayak Tours

CALVERT AND ST. MARY'S COUNTIES

Greenwell State Park
25420 Rosedale Manor Lane
Hollywood MD 20636
301-373-9775
www.dnr.state.md.us/publiclands/southern/greenwell.html
Kayak Rentals, Instruction, Guided Tours

Patuxent Adventure Center
13860 Solomons Island Road
Solomons, MD 20688
410-394-2770
www.paxadventure.com
Kayak Sales, Rentals, Guided Tours

Point Lookout State Park Camp Store
Point Lookout State Park
11175 Point Lookout Road
Scotland, MD 20687
301-872-5688
www.dnr.state.md.us/publiclands/southern/pointlookout.html
Kayak Rentals

LOUDOUN AND FAIRFAX COUNTIES

Blu Gnu Kayak Company
3040 Colvin Street
Alexandria, Virginia 22314
703-751-6662
www.blugnukayak.com
Kayak Instruction, Guided Tours

Canoe Kayak and Paddle Co LLC
2218 Nobehar Drive
Vienna, VA 22181
703-264-8911 (before 9:00 p.m.)
www.ckapco.com
Kayak Instruction, Guided Tours, Instructor Certifications and ACA/BCU
Assessments

Hudson Trail Outfitters, LTD. (HTO)
9488 Fairfax Boulevard
Fairfax, VA 22031
703-591-2950
www.hudsontrail.com
Kayak Sales

Hudson Trail Outfitters, LTD. (HTO)
Springfield Mall
Springfield, VA 22150
703-922-0050
www.hudsontrail.com
Kayak Sales

L.L. Bean
1961 Chain Bridge Road
McLean, VA 22102
703-288-4466
www.llbean.com
Kayak Sales, Instruction

Pohick Bay Regional Park
6501 Pohick Bay Drive
Lorton, VA 22079
703-339-6104
www.nvrpa.org/pohickbay.html
Kayak Rentals, Guided Tours

REI
3509 Carlin Springs Rd
Bailey's Crossroads, VA 22041
703-379-9400
www.rei.com
Kayak Sales

REI
11950 Grand Commons Ave
Fairfax, VA 22030
571-522-6568
www.rei.com
Kayak Sales

PRINCE WILLIAM, STAFFORD AND SPOTSYLVANIA COUNTIES

Clore Bros. Outfitters
5927 River Road
Fredericksburg, VA 22407
540-786-7749
www.clorebros.com
Kayak Rentals

Virginia Outdoor Center
3219 Fall Hill Avenue
Fredericksburg, VA 22401
540-371-5085
www.playva.com
Kayak Rentals, Instruction

PADDLING CLUBS AND ASSOCIATIONS

American Canoe Association
www.americancanoe.org

Canton Kayak Club
www.cantonkayakclub.com

Chesapeake Paddlers Association
www.cpakayaker.com

Greater Baltimore Canoe Club
www.baltimorecanoeclub.org

Monocacy Canoe Club
www.monocacycanoe.org

Delmarva Paddlers
www.groups.yahoo.com/group/delmarvapaddlers

Coastal Canoeists
www.coastals.org

> Maps

Virginia Atlas & Gazetteer, DeLorme Mapping Company,
Freeport, Maine, 1995

Maryland Delaware Atlas & Gazetteer, DeLorme Mapping,
Freeport, Maine, 1993

> References

www.jacksboathouse.com

www.cr.nps.gov

www.dc-movies.com

www.senate.gov

www.bolling.af.mil/index.htm

www.funside.com/

www.saildc.com/

www.fletchersboathouse.com/

www.columbiaisland.com/

www.thompsonboatcenter.com/

www.dnr.state.md.us/publiclands/central/susquehanna.html

www.wtopnews.com

www.constellation.org/

www.cantonkayakclub.com

www.baltimore.org

www.mgs.md.gov/coastal/hmi.html

www.visitbacomd.com/baltimore_county_marinas.cfm

www.wssc.dst.md.us

www.marshypoint.org/

www.wsscwater.com/environment/kidspage/KPFAQS.cfm

www.mdp.state.md.us/

www.mc-mncppc.org/parks/facilities/regional_parks/blackhill/index.shtm

www.hallowedground.org

www.poolesville.com

www.dnr.state.md.us

www.dnr.state.md.us/publiclands/southern/smallwood.html

www.fairfaxcounty.gov/parks/burkelake/marina.htm

www.dgif.virginia.gov/fishing/waterbodies/display.asp?id=17

www.dcr.state.va.us/parks/masonnec.htm

www.dcr.state.va.us/parks/leesylva.htm

www.dcr.state.va.us/parks/parkfees.htm

www.simplyfredericksburg.com

www.harfordcountymd.gov/parks_rec/Parks.cfm?ParkID=48

www.pwcparks.org/lrpark/lrmarina.html

www.annapolis.gov

www.geocities.com/Yosemite/3524/monocacy.html

www.dnr.state.md.us/greenways/charles.html

www.charlescounty.org

www.pgparks.com

www.nps.gov/choh/Recreation/Milepost.html

www.loudounhistory.org

www.potomacriver.org

www.nvrpa.org

www.dcr.state.va.us/parks/masonnec.htm

www.dnr.state.md.us

About the Author

Michaela Gaaserud is a native to the Baltimore/Washington, D.C. area. As a longtime sports writer and outdoor enthusiast, she enjoys distance running, mountain biking, horseback riding, hiking and skiing. An avid sea kayaker and marathon kayak competitor, Michaela has paddled throughout much of the U.S. and Canada including the rugged coast of Nova Scotia, Vancouver Island and the Prince William Sound, Alaska. For nearly a decade, Michaela has been a freelance writer for national paddling publications such as *Canoe & Kayak Magazine* and *Paddler Magazine*.

Michaela is a member of the American Canoe Association, the Chesapeake Paddlers Association and the Adirondack Watershed Alliance.